Be Your Own Coach

Your Pathway to Possibility

Barbara Braham, M.S.W.
Chris Wahl, M.A.Ed.

A Crisp Fifty-Minute™ Series Book

Be Your Own Coach

Your Pathway to Possibility

Barbara Braham, M.S.W.
Chris Wahl, M.A.Ed.

Credits:

VP, Product Development: **Charlie Blum**
Production Editor: **Genevieve McDermott**
Copy Editor: **Charlotte Bosarge**
Production Artists: **Nicole Phillips and Betty Hopkins**

ISBN 10: 1-56052-581-9
ISBN 13: 978-1-56052-581-3
Library of Congress Catalog Card Number 00-102533
Printed in the United States of America

8 9 10 11 12 16 15 14 13

Learning Objectives For:

BE YOUR OWN COACH

The objectives for *Be Your Own Coach* are listed below. They have been developed to guide the user to the core issues covered in this book.

THE OBJECTIVES OF THIS BOOK ARE TO HELP THE USER:

1) Identify coachable moments

2) Discover the benefits and techniques of coaching for self-improvement

3) Reach his or her potential through new perspectives

4) Learn seven coaching tools for achieving breakthroughs

ASSESSING PROGRESS

A Crisp Series **assessment** is available for this book. The 25-item, multiple-choice and true/false questionnaire allows the reader to evaluate his or her comprehension of the subject matter.

To download the assessment and answer key, go to www.axzopress.com and search on the book title.

Assessments should not be used in any employee selection process.

About the Authors

Barbara Braham, MSW, has been awarded the designation of Master Certified Coach by the International Coach Federation. She works with management teams who want to move their organizations forward, and individuals who want to realize their potential. A member of the National Speakers Association, she has delivered hundreds of seminars to audiences across the country on topics such as The Manager as Coach and The Coach Within. She is the author of ten other books, including the Crisp Publications book, *Finding Your Purpose*. You can reach her by email at barbara@bbraham.com, or visit her website BeYourOwnCoach.com.

Chris Wahl, M.A. Ed., has a background in coaching and organization development, and has been awarded the designation of Master Certified Coach by the International Coach Federation. Her international coaching practice focuses on leadership and team excellence. She has been on the faculty of Georgetown University since 1990, has been the Director of the Organization Development Certificate Program there, and has been a featured speaker and author on the integration of coaching and organization development. You can reach her by email at WahlCW@aol.com, or visit her website BeYourOwnCoach.com.

Dedication

This book is dedicated to the memory of Stan Momot and Percy G. Braham, our first teachers in the lesson of believing in our dreams.

To The Reader

We created this book for people who know they can be better employees, managers, colleagues, or leaders. It is for people who are motivated to learn and develop themselves to their full potential. Our intention is to give you concepts and exercises that professional coaches use, so that you can begin the journey of learning more about yourself, especially if you do not wish to hire a coach at this time. As coaches who work every day with people who are pursuing excellence, we know that coaching works. You may decide after going through this book that you would like to have an outside coach, but in the meantime, there are many steps you can take on your own in your quest for excellence. This book is about taking those steps.

If you would like to learn more about coaching yourself, please visit our website at www.BeYourOwnCoach.com. We want to hear your ideas, triumphs, questions, and suggestions. Our website is updated regularly with tips, exercises, and new topics related to personal and professional excellence, and ideas on how you can get the most out of coaching.

Acknowledgments

We would each like to thank our families, Rick Sullivan, and Dan, Jillian, Alexandra, and Carson Wahl, without whose support this book could not have been written. We would also like to thank all of those teachers and colleagues who have contributed to our sense of possibility, especially: Frank Ball, James Flaherty, Sheila Haji, Susana Isaacson, Jacqueline Mandell, Michael Milano, Sandy Mobley, Peter Murphy, John Travis, and Leslie Williams. We gratefully acknowledge our colleagues at Crisp Publications, Debbie Woodbury, Charlotte Bosarge, and Judy Petry for turning our words into these beautiful pages. Lastly, we would like to thank our clients, for you have contributed immensely to this book.

How to Use This Book

As an individual. Set aside time each week, in a quiet place, to do the exercises in this book. We suggest that you purchase a journal with blank pages for you to write, draw, and paste in. When you do the exercises, you will create material about yourself to surface insights and learning, and will begin creating the path for a new way of being.

With a coaching partner. Many people learn best when they can talk about their learning. Each chapter has exercises you can do with a coaching partner. For the purpose of this book, a coaching partner is someone who wants to engage with you in learning. Your coaching partner can work only with you, or you can do the exercises in a reciprocal relationship, walking the learning path together. The sharing that comes out of the paired exercises may bring deeper learning for you both. If you decide to do the exercises with a partner, we have suggestions for you about creating a coaching partnership.

Choosing a Coaching Partner

First, consider who in your life could be in the role of your coaching partner. Find someone who...

➤ Is trustworthy

➤ Will support you (and with whom you can be vulnerable)

➤ Will challenge you

➤ Will listen attentively

➤ Thinks differently from you

➤ Is available to you (you could choose someone who is geographically far from you as long as he or she is available to you)

➤ Would also like to have you as his or her coaching partner (optional)

Then, before completing any exercises in the book, read pages 91–93 about how to have a powerful conversation.

Together...

➤ Talk about what you would like to gain from being in the partnership

➤ Talk about what works best for you in terms of receiving feedback

➤ Talk about the best way you learn and how your partner can help with that

➤ Decide what to do if either of you wants to stop the partnership at anytime

➤ Decide what to do if either of you cannot honor a particular commitment to the other

➤ Set a regular time to meet or talk on the phone

➤ Set a regular time to talk honestly about the partnership experience

Other Ways to Use This Book

Work groups and teams. The exercises in this book can be modified to use in work groups and teams. Groups have breakdowns. Groups have stories. A work group or team could set aside a regular time to explore the need or opportunity for team coaching: after a success, before transitions to new tasks, to periodically examine ways to realize potential, or when there is a breakdown on the team.

Workshops and training programs. This book is an excellent foundation for creating training programs in organizations that want to promote excellence among their employees. The exercises can be modified to fit the needs of organizational learning objectives and can be combined with traditional organization development practices such as action learning and process improvement. A trained facilitator can adapt the exercises within this book to the particular needs of an organization, department, work group, or team.

Study groups. A committed group of people can use the exercises in this book to help each other learn and develop. The book offers a low-cost, structured way to address creating excellence in work and life.

Contents

Introduction

This book offers thought-provoking ideas and valuable tools to help you coach yourself to create more of what you want in your life—your work, your relationships, the many roles that you play. While having a coach can make it easier to commit to excellence, it is possible to dedicate yourself to learning, surround yourself with support systems, and excel, without the benefit of a formal coach. *Be Your Own Coach* will show you how.

Can you benefit from coaching?

To benefit from coaching, you need a commitment and willingness to experiment and learn from what you notice and experience. You need a structure that guides you and helps you make observations about your responses to situations. The commitment comes from you; the structure for the work comes from the book.

So, if you...

➤ Want to be successful in fulfilling new responsibilities

➤ Wish to learn from your successes

➤ Wish to perform more effectively

➤ Feel stuck and unable to see a way out

➤ Would like to chart a new path or want to create better relationships

or have the sense that there is something else, something more natural and more fulfilling, for you to bring your energy to, then coaching can provide you with the environment and tools you need to live your dreams.

Is it really possible to coach yourself?

Yes. We all know people who are excellent in many areas of life who do not have a coach. How do they create and maintain excellence? They read, work on being open-minded, ask for feedback, listen to feedback, take risks, and use every opportunity to learn about themselves in a deep and meaningful way. They are committed. They are purposeful about their quest for excellence.

Are You Coachable?

Read through the following questions and check (✔) the box for each question where you can answer "yes."

Are you:

❏ Committed to your personal and professional development?

❏ A lifelong learner?

❏ Willing to acknowledge where you are stuck in your life?

❏ Open to other ways of seeing the world?

❏ Able to accept feedback?

❏ Willing to try new behaviors?

❏ Willing to reflect on your experience and observe yourself in action?

❏ Willing to develop parts of yourself that may have been neglected?

❏ Willing to challenge your present beliefs?

❏ Willing to begin a relationship with the source of your dissatisfaction?

❏ Willing to consider new possibilities for yourself?

❏ Willing to ask yourself new questions?

❏ Willing to take risks and to change?

❏ Willing to reinvent yourself?

❏ Willing to not know?

❏ Open to ideas other than your own?

❏ Willing to be more authentic in your life?

❏ Willing to experience more purpose and fulfillment?

❏ Willing to let go of behaviors or beliefs that no longer serve you?

❏ Willing to live with uncertainty and ambiguity?

❏ Willing to engage in a process of introspection?

❏ Willing to consider new strategies for success?

If you have eight or more boxes checked "yes" you are ready to benefit from this book. If you have fewer than eight boxes checked, you may get more value from this book by reading it at another time.

PART 1

Openings for Coaching

2

Four Opportunities for Coaching Yourself

How do you know when to coach yourself? There needs to be an opening for coaching. You need to be willing to learn and grow. There are four major times that you can benefit from coaching:

1. **When you receive promotions or new responsibilities**

2. **After a success**

3. **When you want to fulfill more of your potential**

4. **When things go wrong, also known as a "breakdown"**

1 When You Receive Promotions or New Responsibilities

When you step into a new position, or change your job responsibilities, there are opportunities for you to learn, and many openings for coaching. People who use new responsibilities as an opening for coaching learn more than the technical aspects of the new job. A coaching approach invites you to learn about how you learn, to explore how you handle your feelings of doubt and uncertainty in a new role, and to notice the way you develop relationships in your new role. In short, coaching takes a holistic view to changing job responsibilities and helps you step into all the possibilities that such a change presents.

2 After a Success

Too often we fail to celebrate our successes. And too often we fail to learn from our successes. It is easy to quickly rush on to the next project. When you experience success on a project, with a customer or co-worker, or within yourself, this is an opening for coaching. A coaching approach helps you look at your success with an eye to how you can repeat the success in diverse situations. A coaching approach helps you identify what you did, and how you acted that led to the success.

3 When You Want to Fulfill More of Your Potential

There are so many possibilities in the world! Possibilities to learn new things, meet new people, take risks, explore new behaviors. If you find yourself wanting to grow personally and or professionally, coaching is an excellent way to do it. You can coach yourself to be prepared for new opportunities at your workplace. You do not need to wait for a new job to learn new skills. You can prepare yourself for leadership roles in your personal and professional life before you step into those roles. Coaching is a tool that builds self-confidence, personal responsibility, and excellence.

Openings for coaching are around you all the time. You need to learn to see them. They show up at work, with your friends, in your family, in your professional associations—everywhere. The greater your commitment to lifelong learning, the more easily you will notice openings for coaching. Openings are your personal invitations to coach yourself.

4 When Things Go Wrong or When There Is a Breakdown

As you move through your life, there will be times when everything goes great. And there will be times when things do not go the way you want them to. Times when you do not get the outcome that you want, times when you feel embarrassed, inadequate, or stuck. Times of opportunity, like leading a special project, when you are not prepared. Times when you make a big mistake. Times when you think to yourself—"Uh Oh."

If you find yourself saying…

"Uh oh, this team meeting is off on a tangent again" (and you're the meeting facilitator)

"Oh no, I'm not going to make this deadline" (and you promised your boss you would)

"Oops, this client isn't going to renew their contract with us" (and your company is counting on that sale)

"Yipes, I don't know how to do this" (and you're the person people look to for technical expertise)

"Oh dear, there's a lot of distance in this relationship" (and you need to work closely with this person, or maybe you live with the person)

…then you are facing a breakdown. When facing a breakdown, a coaching approach views the breakdown as an opportunity for you to learn, to try new ways of managing a problem. Breakdown situations always offer an opening for coaching that may lead to a richer, more competent way of being and living.

Examples of Coaching Openings

Promotions or a Change in Responsibilities

➤ You have been promoted into managing a large number of people

➤ You have been promoted from a technical to a leadership position

➤ You have been reorganized into a new position, with new reporting lines

➤ You have been demoted

After a Success

➤ You have landed a huge contract

➤ You have saved a major client account

➤ Your team exceeded all of its goals

➤ You have been given an award for excellent performance

When You Want to Fulfill Your Potential

➤ You know you can move into a management position and want to chart a path towards that

➤ You know you can coach others around you to be leaders but you don't know where to start

➤ You want to share your recent learning experiences with others

➤ You have great ideas but aren't confident to speak up in meetings

When Things Go Wrong or There Is a Breakdown

➤ Your management style doesn't match the style of your subordinates

➤ You can't seem to communicate with your boss

➤ You have an employee who promises one thing and delivers another

➤ You are angry that you were passed over for promotion

➤ You take on too many projects and miss more deadlines than you make

➤ You have a hard time being a team player

YOUR COACHING OPPORTUNITIES

What openings for coaching are there in your life right now? Write your answer here or in your coaching journal.

_____

_____

_____

_____

_____

_____

_____

With a coaching partner

Take up to five minutes each, to describe an opening for coaching yourself to the other. Do not use this time to "fix," "offer advice," or otherwise "help" your partner. Just listen.

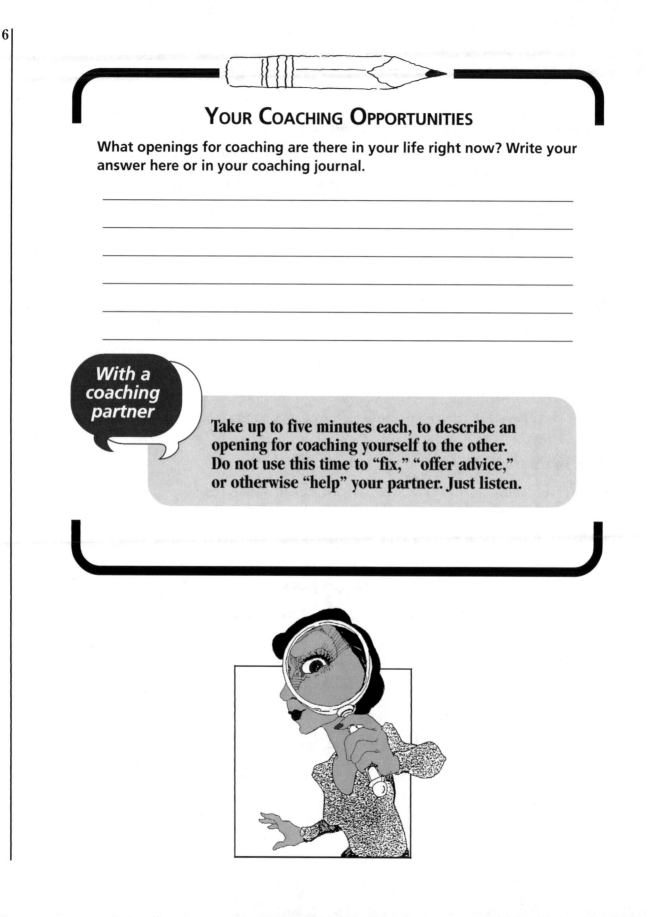

Signs that You've Missed a Coaching Opening

To successfully be your own coach, you need to notice openings for coaching. You need to practice noticing when things are going right, when things aren't going right, when there is an inner call to be more of who you are, or when there is something you need to learn. If you don't pay attention, you can miss an opening for coaching.

Here are some of the ways you can miss an opening. Watch for these in your life.

1 Denial or Ignoring an Opening

Some people move rapidly from awareness into denial. For example, in a breakdown situation you might think to yourself, "Oh no, this meeting isn't going very well. We're off on a tangent (awareness). But, it's good to let people express their opinions. It's okay (denial)." Things stay the way they are. You don't make any changes in your behavior. Or, in the case of a promotion, you ignore the skills you don't have and keep doing your "old" job with the new title.

2 Resignation

Some people resign themselves to living the same experiences again and again. They don't believe they have the power to change. They don't see their potential and the possibilities before them. If this describes you, you may want to consider hiring a coach to help you see things differently.

3 Blame

Some people move from seeing an opening into blaming. If something goes wrong, it is the fault of a manager, a co-worker, the organization, the weather, their computer, etc., that the breakdown is occurring. As long as you find ways to blame, you keep yourself from accepting any responsibility or taking any action. The result: No learning takes place. No personal growth. No development.

People struggling with new job responsibilities sometimes find it easier to blame others for their moments of doubt than to coach themselves through it. Sometimes people blame others for being "difficult" instead of developing their own interpersonal skills.

4 Self-Recrimination

Some people beat themselves up with their self-talk. They say things to themselves like:

"It's always my fault."

"What's wrong with me?"

"Why can't I get it right?"

"Why don't I know more?"

"Why can't I do this?"

"Anybody could have done this. It's no big deal."

Negative self-talk prevents you from seeing the opening for coaching. You get stuck inside your own mind and lose the opportunity for personal and professional growth.

Seize any opening for coaching! Don't let it pass you by. Use this book to turn your coachable moments into learning opportunities.

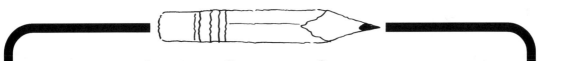

IDENTIFY COACHING OPENINGS

For the next two weeks, pay attention to the coaching openings in your life. How do you respond to them? This is not an exercise for judgment. It is an exercise for observation. You want to notice if you approach your coachable moments in the same way, use a specific approach for certain situations, or respond in a variety of different ways. Use your journal or the space below to write down coachable moments that you noticed and how you responded to them.

_____

_____

_____

_____

_____

_____

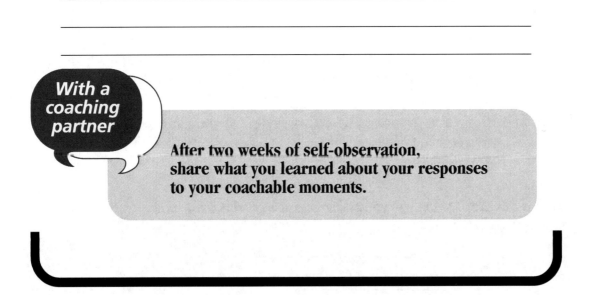

With a coaching partner

After two weeks of self-observation, share what you learned about your responses to your coachable moments.

The Coaching Approach

If you're going to be your own coach, then you need to get into the habit of noticing your opportunities—or openings—for coaching. These coachable moments can then become invitations into a breakthrough. If you learn to apply the coaching approach, any of the four types of coaching openings mentioned earlier have the potential to break you open to a new way of seeing, doing, or experiencing life. They don't have to break you down.

When You Receive a Promotion or New Responsibilities

STEP 1: Identify what you don't know. This is called a gap analysis. In one column on the left-hand side of a page in your journal, make a list of the skills you need to successfully perform in your new role. Then, on the right-hand side, list your present skills. The difference between the two lists is your gap and learning opportunity. If you are not sure what skills you need, ask your coaching partner, boss, or a co-worker.

STEP 2: Ask yourself who or what can help you close the gap. Is there a person who can coach you? Do you need to take a course or read a book?

STEP 3: Notice your personal learning style. Do you embrace new learning? Are you feeling resistant? Do you feel vulnerable about what you don't know? Do you want to avoid what you don't know?

STEP 4: Evaluate. Review your progress on a regular basis in closing the gap you identified in Step 1.

After a Success

STEP 1: Set aside time to reflect on the success. Ask yourself what made the situation a success. For example, was it your organizational skills, your technical expertise, your knowledge base, the team of people you selected, the timing, your communication skills, the synergies created by several of these, or something else? Too often we don't take the time to find out what made something work.

STEP 2: Ask yourself if the success factor could be strengthened. How could you develop it to an even higher level?

STEP 3: Ask yourself where else you could apply this success factor. Are there other projects or relationships that would benefit if you brought this success factor to them?

STEP 4: Think about who needs to learn this success skill. Who might you mentor or coach so that they might experience the kinds of successes you've just experienced? This last point creates a culture for coaching within your organization.

If You Want to Fulfill More of Your Personal Potential

These steps are slightly different. Begin by making a list of your gifts or talents. What are the things that you do well naturally? Ask friends if you are not sure. How could you enhance those gifts with new skills? For example, if you have a gift for creating a climate of trust, would facilitation skills, conflict management skills, or communication skills strengthen this talent? Would these skills give you new ways to use your talent?

Next, look over your list and ask yourself which of these gifts are not being expressed in your current work situation. You might fulfill more of your potential if you could find ways to use these gifts in the workplace. Make a list of ways that you could bring unused talents into your work.

The last step is to create a plan. Will you expand your talents with new skills? Or will you find ways to bring more of who you are into your daily work?

When Things Go Wrong or There Is a Breakdown

Of the four openings to coaching, perhaps the most difficult is the breakdown. Let's take a deeper look at how to turn a breakdown into a coachable moment.

Breakdowns are caused in part by the inability to see possibilities in the situation. That leads you to pull back and feel stressed in the situation. Instead, your goal is to feel open and relaxed. When you feel open, creativity can enter. If you're in a breakdown, then by definition what you're doing isn't working. You need a new approach. You need to be creative.

To turn a breakdown into a coachable moment, it is important to resist the tendency to identify with the breakdown. This means that *you are not your breakdown*. If you can separate yourself from the breakdown, you will be able to take a very important step: asking for help.

CASE STUDY: APARNA

ABC Company had employees spread out across the state. When training was offered it required many people to travel to a central location. This worked for a full-day training session, but if a training program required less than a full day, the travel time and costs were prohibitive. Consequently, training sessions were scheduled for full days whether the subject needed it or not. This created frustration and dissatisfaction among the trainees. A breakdown occurred for Aparna, the training manager, when a particular course was needed that was best delivered in 90-minute modules over 10 weeks. The only option she could see was not to offer the course. But the company had determined the course was a high priority. As Aparna shared her breakdown with others, new options emerged: hold the training at multiple sites, invest in videoconferencing, set up a virtual classroom through teleclasses or produce an audio course.

Asking for help goes counter to a common bias towards self-reliance, independence, and heroism. Movies traditionally show heroes who figure things out on their own and solve their own problems. But these movies no longer reflect the reality that we live in. In the 21st century, interdependence is the hallmark of those who will be most successful.

What kind of help are you asking for? The first type of help you want is fresh eyes. You want the perspective of someone who sees the world (or at least your situation) differently than you do. You need more options, more choices. Ask yourself, who can offer you "fresh eyes" on your breakdown?

The second type of help you may need is specific expertise. In the previous example, Aparna didn't know how to set up a bridge line for a teleclass. She had no experience with videoconferencing. She was able to identify people who were familiar with these technologies and learn how she could apply them in her company. Her breakdown led to a breakthrough in how the company delivered training to a geographically dispersed workforce. Ask yourself who has the expertise to help you with your breakdown.

Important Note: If you are in a supervisory or managerial role in your organization, part of your job is to identify breakdowns. That is how the organization will continue to thrive in changing conditions. Too often, supervisors and managers perceive a breakdown as a threat to their competence and try to keep the breakdown a secret. This is a great disservice to the organization and the individual.

Breakdowns and Interconnection

After you've asked for help and found some creative possibilities for yourself, you then need to consider the impact of your breakdown.

Nothing occurs in isolation. All of life is interconnected. Every behavior is the cause or condition for other behaviors. To maximize the learning in a breakdown, you need to consider the impact of the breakdown on people, systems, and commitments.

CASE STUDY: LUCAS

Lucas was chairing a team meeting when he lost his temper, and yelled at several of his team members in front of the others. The first time this occurred he denied that it was anything to be concerned about. The second time it occurred, he felt shame and criticized himself for not having better self-control. Several months later, when it occurred a third time, he viewed it as a breakdown and began to assess the real impact of his behavior.

Assessing Lucas's Breakdown

Consider the impact of Lucas's behavior by answering the following questions:

1. **Who stands to suffer or benefit as a result of the breakdown?**

   _____

2. **Who needs to know about this breakdown?**

   _____

3. **What systems will be affected by this breakdown?**

   _____

   _____

4. **What schedules will be delayed as a result of this breakdown?**

   _____

   _____

5. **What will Lucas be unable to do that he promised to do as a result of this breakdown?**

   _____

   _____

Compare your answers with the authors' on the following page.

CASE STUDY ANSWERS

1. Who stands to suffer or benefit as a result of the breakdown?

All the people on the team are now fearful to express their true views for fear that Lucas will lose his temper. After the meeting is over they hold the "meeting after the meeting" to talk about what happened. This reduces their productivity. Some of these conversations are held with people who were not in the meeting, which leads to rumors.

2. Who needs to know about this breakdown?

Lucas's boss will hear the rumors in the hallways. Therefore, Lucas needs to tell his boss before the boss hears the rumors. Lucas would benefit from talking this situation over with a coach or a coaching partner to prepare himself for the conversation with his boss.

3. What systems will be affected by this breakdown?

Lucas's behavior is undermining the company's initiative for teamwork. Members of the team do not feel it is safe to express their opinions. They begin to wait to be told what to do rather than initiate action. People in other departments who hear about Lucas's hot temper decide not to bring sensitive issues to him. Information flow is seriously disrupted as a result.

4. What schedules will be delayed as a result of this breakdown?

The team's work is behind schedule. As a result, there is another department that will not get the data they expected on time.

5. What will Lucas be unable to do that he promised to do as a result of this breakdown?

As the team leader, Lucas is responsible for providing leadership, acting as a role model, and ensuring that the team fulfills its mission. His behavior is undermining his ability to lead and is jeopardizing the team's success. Therefore, his breakdown is likely to prevent him from delivering on his leadership promise. In addition, Lucas's confidence is so shaken that he is having difficulty focusing on other commitments he has made; he cancels his afternoon meetings, calls home and leaves a message for his daughter that he will miss her soccer game that evening. Therefore, systems that have depended on him pay the price for his breakdown.

Failure to see the interconnectedness of all things may add unnecessary suffering to an already painful situation.

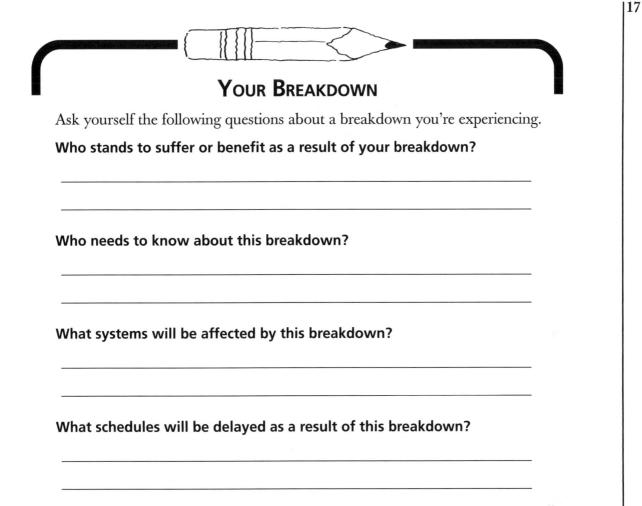

YOUR BREAKDOWN

Ask yourself the following questions about a breakdown you're experiencing.

Who stands to suffer or benefit as a result of your breakdown?

_____

_____

Who needs to know about this breakdown?

_____

_____

What systems will be affected by this breakdown?

_____

_____

What schedules will be delayed as a result of this breakdown?

_____

_____

What are you unable to do that you promised to do because of this breakdown?

_____

_____

With a coaching partner

Answer the above questions together. Ask your partner to bring fresh eyes to your situation. Would he or she add anything to your answers? Does your partner see anything you missed?

18

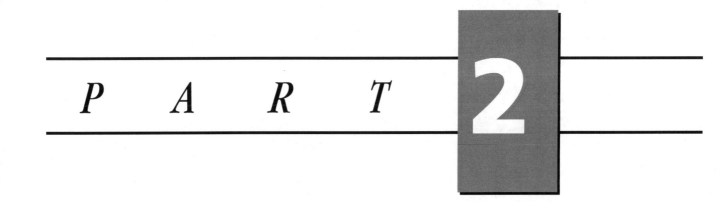

In the Middle of This Road You Call Your Life

How Did You Get Where You Are?

At this moment you are in the middle of all the commitments you've already made—mortgage, kids, car payments, etc. You have made decisions that closed some paths and opened others. Some of the doors you closed can never be opened again. Other closed doors could be revisited in the future. If you are a 50-year-old woman who chose not to bear children, that door probably can't be opened. However, if you didn't get a college degree and now you are 55, you can still go back to school.

Over the years you have entered into relationships that both enriched you and diminished you. You have made wise and unwise financial decisions that impact how you now live your life. You have made choices about your health (smoking, drinking, lying in the sun, diet) and they may be affecting you now or will in the future. You have taken jobs you loved and stayed in jobs that robbed you of your soul. You've felt the full range of human emotions at one time or another and decided to embrace them or cut them off.

Events and experiences in your life have shaped your beliefs. Some of these beliefs have solidified into "truths" that limit you; some have solidified into "truths" that blind you. Some of your beliefs empower you; some weaken you.

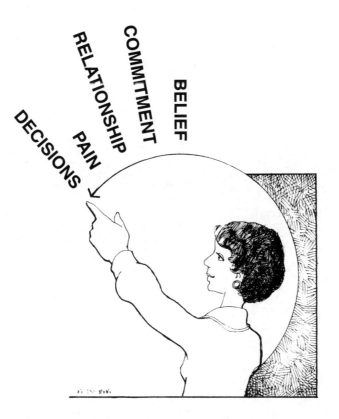

You are not a blank slate. Life has written all over you. Consequently, there are some things that don't seem to be options for you. There are some things that you simply don't see. However, there is another truth here. Options abound. It is because you have already made so many commitments that you feel stuck at times. Your life has a momentum of its own that at times can run you right into a wall. Breakdowns can occur anytime, anywhere, but without creating a context for your breakdown, it is difficult, if not impossible, to see new possibilities.

THE CIRCLE OF LIFE

This exercise is designed to help you see the interconnections in your life and how your past decisions, feelings, relationships, and commitments have made an impact on who you are today.

Make a list of five significant decision points in your life. One way to identify these is to think about significant emotional events in your life. What decisions did you make as a result of those events? What were the results of your decisions?

Significant emotional events	Decision made	Results of the decision
Examples:		
Major illness	Work less, spend time with family	Less stress, improved family life
Job loss	Save 10% of income	Financial nest egg

1. _____

2. _____

3. _____

4. _____

5. _____

Make a list of five situations when you felt a strong feeling—positive or negative. How did you deal with the feeling? Did you face it, distract yourself from it (using busyness, shopping, alcohol etc.), deny it, try to hold on to it, feel deserving or undeserving?

The feeling	How I responded
Examples:	
Grief	Got busy
Joy	Felt undeserving, sabotaged it

(CONTINUED)

The feeling	How I responded
1. _____	
2. _____	
3. _____	
4. _____	
5. _____	

Make a list of five significant relationships (past and present) in your life. Consider family, friends, teachers, co-workers, bosses, causes, and institutions when you make your list. What conclusions do you come to about yourself in the context of these relationships?

Relationship	How the relationship serves me	What part of me is expressed in the relationship?
Examples:		
Boss	Learned lots	Risk taker, learner
Professional association	Networking	Contributor, outgoing
1. _____		
2. _____		
3. _____		
4. _____		
5. _____		

(CONTINUED)

(CONTINUED)

Make a list of five current commitments. Note your relationship to that commitment. In other words, do you dread it, resent it, enjoy it, learn from it, cherish it, try to avoid it, etc. How were those commitments made? (Conscious choice? Unconscious choice? Resignation? Fear? Guilt? The easy way out? Greed? Anger?)

Commitments	My relationship to the commitment	How I made the commitment
Examples:		
Daily exercise	Enjoy	Health fears, conscious choice
Chair giving campaign	Resent	Guilt, felt pressured

1. _____

   _____

2. _____

   _____

3. _____

   _____

4. _____

   _____

5. _____

   _____

The answers to these questions are the fabric of the tapestry you call your life. Notice how they are interrelated. Can you see the causes and conditions that have put you where you are in your life at this moment? Be aware that the decisions, feelings, commitments, and relationships of today are creating the life you will be in the middle of tomorrow.

What Is Your Story?

Coachable moments are an integral part of your life. In fact, it is the context of your life that shapes the openings that are uniquely yours. Can you see your successes? Do you believe you have potential? How do you view a coachable moment? What is your response to new responsibilities? In other words: What's your story? We all have created stories about our lives, about what has happened to us. Stories can limit us and keep us stuck or expand us by creating possibility.

Think of the answer to this question the way a movie producer thinks of a movie. In other words, are you living any of these story lines?

"Boy meets girl, they fall in love and live happily ever after"

"Life is a struggle"

"When bad things happen to good people"

"Rags to riches"

"Life is a cosmic joke"

"Victim"

"If you can dream it you can live it"

TESTING YOUR VIEWS

Read the description of each coaching opening and check (✔) whether the stories are limiting or creating possibilities.

Opening: You are unhappy in your job. You dread going to work and feel stressed. Your health is being affected.

The life you are in the middle of: You are a single parent struggling to raise your kids and make ends meet.

Story 1: You believe the job market is good now and would like to try for a better job.

❏ Limiting   ❏ Creating Possibility

Story 2: If only your boss would transfer, you would be happy.

❏ Limiting   ❏ Creating Possibility

Story 3: Changing jobs is always risky.

❏ Limiting   ❏ Creating Possibility

Story 4: You can see ways to expand yourself on the job and want to bring this up to your boss.

❏ Limiting   ❏ Creating Possibility

Story 5: You have skills you aren't using and believe there is a job out there that will use all that you have, and pay you accordingly.

❏ Limiting   ❏ Creating Possibility

Story 6: You are angry with your parents for not giving you help so that you don't have to struggle so much.

❏ Limiting   ❏ Creating Possibility

Story 7 : You'd like to take some courses to build your skills and increase your marketability.

❏ Limiting   ❏ Creating Possibility

Compare your responses with the authors' on the next page.

AUTHORS' RESPONSES: TESTING YOUR VIEWS

1. **Creating Possibility.** Optimism and a willingness to learn are present in this story.

2. **Limiting.** Blaming someone outside for your happiness limits your ability to find happiness, and puts control with someone else—your boss.

3. **Limiting.** Without even exploring the extent of the risk of changing job, you are taking on an attitude of resignation, and you will not see possibilities.

4. **Creating Possibility.** You are proactively exploring ways to take care of yourself and bring your best forward.

5. **Creating Possibility.** You are optimistic and believe in yourself. Great combination.

6. **Limiting.** Blaming your parents for not helping you keeps you locked in anger and prohibits your ability to create a new way of seeing the situation.

7. **Creating Possibility.** You are finding ways to get better, and taking this on as your responsibility.

Each story holds within it different possibilities, threats, and potential for learning. As humans, we are subject to the stories we create about our situations. Getting caught in the same script is what keeps you stuck. That is why "fresh eyes" are important to help you see how you are limiting yourself.

WHAT'S YOUR STORY?

In an earlier exercise, Your Coaching Opportunities (page 6), you took the time to describe an opening that you are currently experiencing. Reread what you wrote there, then answer the questions, either here or in your journal.

What story are you telling yourself about this opening?

_____

_____

_____

_____

How is the story limiting you?

_____

_____

_____

_____

Where are the possibilities in your story?

_____

_____

_____

_____

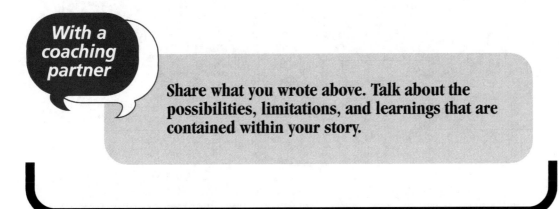

With a coaching partner

Share what you wrote above. Talk about the possibilities, limitations, and learnings that are contained within your story.

The Kaleidoscope View of Life

You've no doubt seen the picture where, depending upon how you look at it, there is an old woman or a young woman. Or, if not that one, you've seen the picture that if viewed one way reveals two faces looking in opposite directions, but if seen another way shows a chalice. These graphic images dramatize that there is more than one way to view a situation.

In the case of your life, you have a kaleidoscope of choices for how you see it. If you've looked through a kaleidoscope, then you know that with one turn you see red and blue, with another turn green shows up, with still another purple appears, and with each turn the shapes and perspectives change.

When you coach yourself, it is critical that you recognize that how you perceive a situation depends upon which lens you use. Feeling stuck is frequently the result of turning the kaleidoscope only once and thinking there is no view other than the first one. In tough situations, you need to identify the facts so you are able to turn through each of these lenses to see more choices.

Identifying the Facts

Most people find it very difficult to observe a situation and tell the bare facts. Instead, what come out are assumptions, interpretations, and judgments all dressed up as if they are "facts" or the "truth." The facts describe what is without anything added.

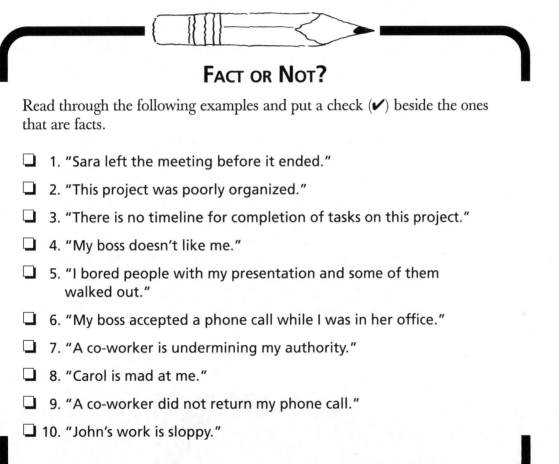

FACT OR NOT?

Read through the following examples and put a check (✔) beside the ones that are facts.

❑ 1. "Sara left the meeting before it ended."

❑ 2. "This project was poorly organized."

❑ 3. "There is no timeline for completion of tasks on this project."

❑ 4. "My boss doesn't like me."

❑ 5. "I bored people with my presentation and some of them walked out."

❑ 6. "My boss accepted a phone call while I was in her office."

❑ 7. "A co-worker is undermining my authority."

❑ 8. "Carol is mad at me."

❑ 9. "A co-worker did not return my phone call."

❑ 10. "John's work is sloppy."

Questions #1,3,6,9 are facts.

Your Feelings

Most people have a limited vocabulary when it comes to naming their feelings. It is easy to get the major feelings: angry, sad, happy, scared. You may even have a second tier of "feeling" words in your vocabulary such as depressed, irritated, frustrated, excited, and anxious. But how many other feeling words do you know?

To be your own coach, it is critical that you learn to distinguish among a wide variety of feelings. The finer your distinctions, the more choices you will have in a situation—the more colors you will have in your kaleidoscope. For example, can you distinguish between miffed, peeved, angry, perturbed, and furious? If you have only one word for all the shades of a feeling, your kaleidoscope has fewer colors in it.

Knowledgeable experts in any field have the ability to make distinctions that non-experts can't see. For example, you can look at the ocean and see waves, big ones and little ones. A sailor looking at the ocean can see currents, waves, and signals from the water and wind that a non-sailor would never notice. One of the reasons people seek out a coach or a mentor is for the distinctions that person can provide. As your own coach, you will need to develop the capacity to distinguish among many subtle feelings. If you've had trouble in the past identifying your feelings, it may not be that you're "out of touch" with your feelings. Rather, it may be that you simply lack the words to define what you feel. Consequently you may conclude that you don't know what you feel.

EXPANDING YOUR KALEIDOSCOPE

Look through the list of feeling words on the following pages. Put a line through the feeling words that you use regularly. The words that remain are your opportunity for learning. Go through the remaining words one by one and recall a situation when you felt that feeling. Your purpose in doing this exercise is to begin to expand your ability to identify and name a broad range of feelings.

With a coaching partner. Review page 6 where you wrote out your coaching opportunity and page 29 where you wrote the story around it. Using the list of feeling words, identify all of your feelings in the situation. Try not to use the feeling words that you put a line through. Use this exercise to practice finding new words to express your feelings.

As you become more skillful at naming your feelings, you will discover that they change–sometimes rapidly. Their intensity ebbs and flows. At times they dissolve on their own. Your challenge is to relate *to* your feelings and not *from* your feelings. In other words, if you feel angry, you don't want to respond to someone from the place of feeling angry. Instead, your goal is to identify the feeling of anger and decide how to best express it in a given moment–you relate *to* the anger. You care for yourself and your feelings by honoring them, yet not being run by them.

Abandoned
Absorbed
Accepted
Accomplished
Adored
Adrift
Affectionate
Afraid
Aggravated
Agitated
Alert
Alive
Amazed
Ambivalent
Apathetic
Appalled
Appreciative
Argumentative
Aroused
Ashamed
Bashful
Belittled
Belligerent
Benevolent
Betrayed
Bitter
Blue
Bummed
Cantankerous
Capable
Carefree
Careless
Cavalier
Certain
Chagrined
Charitable
Cherished
Circumspect
Coerced

Combative
Committed
Compassionate
Competent
Compliant
Composed
Concerned
Condemned
Confident
Conspicuous
Contemplative
Contentious
Contrite
Courageous
Cowardly
Crazy
Curious
Cynical
Daunted
Deceived
Dedicated
Defeated
Defensive
Defiant
Dejected
Delighted
Demure
Depleted
Depressed
Deprived
Derided
Deserving
Desirable
Despair
Despondent
Devoted
Disappointed
Disconcerted
Discontent

Disconnected
Discouraged
Disdainful
Disheartened
Disheveled
Disillusioned
Disingenuous
Disparaged
Dumbfounded
Duped
Eager
Ecstatic
Effective
Embarrassed
Empty
Encouraged
Energetic
Engaged
Elated
Emasculated
Enlightened
Enriched
Enthralled
Entrusted
Envious
Excluded
Exhausted
Exhilarated
Exonerated
Exposed
Fantastic
Flustered
Foolish
Forgiving
Forsaken
Frantic
Friendly
Frisky
Fulfilled

Furious
Generous
Gentle
Giving
Gloomy
Grateful
Guarded
Guilty
Gullible
Happy
Hateful
Healthy
Heartbroken
Helpful
Helpless
Hopeful
Hopeless
Horrible
Humble
Humiliated
Hurt
Hypocritical
Ignorant
Ignored
Impaired
Impassioned
Impassive
Impatient
Imperfect
Imperiled
Important
Impressed
Impudent
Impulsive
Inadequate
Indecisive
Indifferent
Indignant
Inferior

Infuriated	Miserly	Preoccupied	Sheepish
Ingenuous	Misunderstood	Pretentious	Shocked
Inquisitive	Mixed Up	Productive	Selfish
Insecure	Modest	Proud	Sensitive
Insolent	Moody	Puzzled	Serene
Intense	Morose	Quiet	Serious
Intimidated	Naïve	Reactive	Slighted
Intolerant	Neglected	Reassured	Smart
Intrepid	Nervous	Reborn	Smug
Introverted	Nonplused	Recalcitrant	Silly
Invisible	Numb	Receptive	Sincere
Invulnerable	Obligated	Reflective	Sorry
Irresponsible	Offended	Refreshed	Spent
Irked	Open	Regretful	Splendid
Jaded	Opposed	Rejected	Squashed
Jealous	Ornery	Relaxed	Stifled
Jolly	Overjoyed	Reliable	Stingy
Joyful	Overwhelmed	Remorse	Stretched
Jubilant	Pampered	Reproved	Strong
Judgmental	Paranoid	Resentful	Stupid
Jumpy	Passionate	Reserved	Suffocated
Kind	Passive	Resistant	Sullen
Knowledgeable	Patient	Resolute	Surly
Lazy	Patronized	Respected	Surprised
Leery	Peaceful	Responsible	Suspicious
Lethargic	Peeved	Restrained	Sympathetic
Light-hearted	Pensive	Reverent	Tender
Listless	Perplexed	Ridiculous	Thrilled
Loathsome	Perturbed	Right	Thoughtful
Lonely	Pessimistic	Rigid	Thwarted
Lost	Petrified	Rotten	Trapped
Lousy	Petulant	Rushed	Troubled
Loving	Pious	Sad	Understood
Lucky	Playful	Sassy	Uneasy
Mad	Pompous	Scared	Valued
Melancholy	Positive	Scolded	Victimizes
Merry	Pouty	Scrutinized	Wary
Miffed	Powerful	Secure	Welcome
Miserable	Precocious	Shamed	Withdrawn

Your Moods

Some days you wake up in a "good mood." You are ready to take on the day, believe you can handle anything that comes your way, and smile all the way through. Nothing can get to you on those days! You are productive, people want to be around you, you notice the beauty around you, and live life in a spirit of gratefulness.

Other days, you wake up grouchy, or tired, or pessimistic. Your energy is low and nothing you do helps. You begin to believe that people are doing and saying things just to get on your nerves. You can't concentrate and can only think about relieving your angst, vague as it may be. Maybe if you could take a nap, things would get better. Or eat a cookie. Or tell someone off. Or have a drink. Or hide. We have all experienced days when the veil of doom descends, just as we have experienced days when the veil of doom does not exist. But are these your moods? No.

What we have described above are feelings, which, as you know, don't last.

Feelings pass. They change, often very quickly. *But our moods prevail.* Our moods are so much a part of us that we may not even see them. They shape how we see the world. They shape how we react to words, people, and events. The people with whom you interact can often predict your response to something because they have observed and learned about your prevailing mood.

Optimism and Pessimism

In his book, *Learned Optimism* (NY: Pocket Books, 1998), Martin E. P. Seligman declares that optimism can be learned, and that you can alter your moods by learning to think differently. There are people who are suffering because they habitually choose a pessimistic view. That view affects their energy, relationships, sense of purpose, and sense of self.

While optimism and pessimism are overarching moods, other moods can strongly affect workplace behavior, such as those listed below.

Are you...

Accepting   Fearful   Friendly   Grateful   Inferior   Resigned   Superior   Angry

Each of the above moods has observable behaviors. An over-inflated ego can lead to controlling, competing, or disrespectful behaviors aimed at keeping the person feeling on top, or "Superior" to others. Or, the mood of "Accepting" can provide the chance for open dialogue, respectful actions, or creativity.

Negative Moods

Negative moods are those moods which cause you to routinely see the world in a pessimistic light. A caution here. This does not mean that a person should never be negative! There are times when raising the counteropinion, being a skeptic, or not trusting are exactly the right ways to be. They can keep you from rash acts. However, to live in negativity, to respond to the world with negativity, to live in the mood of pessimism—all of these have consequences.

First, a negative mood creates thoughts that take up brain space that could be used more productively. Think about it. What would happen if you cleared your brain of pessimism? Of needing to be right? Of looking for the negative?

A second consequence of a negative mood is that it creates situations for you where it takes tremendous energy to hold your position on an issue, event, or circumstance. Have you ever held such a strong position that you ended up spending enormous, often angry, energy rebuking any evidence that is contrary to that position? This is a waste of energy that is meaningless to everyone except you.

The third consequence is that a negative mood cuts off possibilities, and you are the one who pays for that.

Remember, the mood that you live in is like a suit of clothes. And like a suit of clothes, you *can* choose to wear something new and different. You can learn about your usual ways of viewing the world and the mood that shapes your view. And, you can choose to think about yourself in a new and different way, which changes your mood and the way that you interact with the world.

UNDERSTANDING MOODS

Here or in your journal, answer the following questions aimed at helping you determine mood, using the moods listed on pages 34-35.

1. Think of someone in your life whose reactions are predictable.

_____

_____

2. How would you describe the mood they "live" in?

_____

_____

3. How does it offer possibilities to them?

_____

_____

4. How does it cut off possibilities for them?

_____

_____

5. How is their mood expressed through their words and actions?

_____

_____

6. How do you think someone would answer these questions about you?

_____

_____

GATHERING FEEDBACK ON YOUR MOOD

Choose three people who know you well and ask them for feedback on your general mood. Invite them to be honest with you and let them know you are grateful for their honesty. Be a spacious listener—that is, be open enough to listen, even if you disagree with the feedback you are receiving. If you invite feedback, it is up to you to hear it and create the space for the speaker to give you feedback. Otherwise, they will be unlikely to give you feedback in the future. You may wish to record their feedback, and your reactions to it, in your journal.

Talk to your coaching partner about the feedback you received. Share your moods. Brainstorm ways to alter any moods that are not helpful. Support each other in making new choices about your moods.

Your Words Create Your Reality

One of the keys to becoming more fulfilled is to notice how your words create your reality. Negative words that you say to yourself lead to a negative interpretation of an event. A negative interpretation gives you fewer options. Positive words based on optimism give you more options. Consider these interpretations in response to the following situation.

CASE STUDY: CALVIN

Calvin, the team leader of a successful product development team learns that one the team's key players, Cheryl, has recently applied to move to another team, right in the middle of the product development cycle. Calvin is extremely disappointed at losing a key player at such a critical time in the team's work. Relationships on this team have been friendly and productive. Calvin could think any of the following:

1. Cheryl is fundamentally unhappy with Calvin's approach to leading the team (personalizing/blaming himself for the event).

2. Cheryl is valuable to the organization and will bring great skill to the new team, so wherever she goes, she is an asset (accepting/recognizing that nothing is forever).

3. Cheryl is trying to undermine the team's efforts by leaving (attributing negative intention/thinking the team member is against the team).

4. Cheryl sees a great opportunity for advancement by going to the new team (possibility she is taking care of herself and her career).

Consider which of the preceeding responses create the most possibility in terms of

➤ Calvin's relationship with himself

➤ Calvin's relationship with Cheryl

➤ Calvin's ability to move on from his disappointment

Clearly, the more one tends to interpret events from a negative viewpoint, the less chance there is to have open conversation about any event. And the more that negative thoughts occupy you, the less chance you have of seeing any other possibilities besides the negative story you are telling yourself.

So, in this situation, what could Calvin do?

❏ Accept it. (Recognize that others have choices.)

❏ Ask himself what he needs to know to feel okay with this change, and then act on it. For example, Calvin may talk with Cheryl about her decision to join another team. (Open a conversation to learn the reason for the change.)

❏ Wish Cheryl well. (Decide that a conversation isn't necessary but that encouragement fits with the view Calvin has of himself.)

❏ Create a good-bye meeting to acknowledge Cheryl's good work and to allow other team members to acknowledge her contribution to the team effort. (Create a positive atmosphere regarding Cheryl's departure).

❏ Get cranky and depressed. (Blame his bad mood on Cheryl.)

❏ Quit as team leader. (Decide that he's a lousy team leader and give it up altogether.)

It is important here to note that the actual event is neutral until Calvin begins to interpret the event through his lens for seeing the world. The same is true with events that happen in our lives: by themselves, they mean nothing. *Only when we interpret them do they take on meaning.*

Now it is time to examine your reactions and to learn more about how your words and your interpretations create reality for you.

42

EXAMINING YOUR REACTIONS AND WORDS

In your journal, describe an event that upset you. Describe your reaction to it. What did you think, feel, say, do?

With a coaching partner

Share what you wrote with your coaching partner. See if you can help each other uncover your interpretations and determine how they affected your words and reactions. Use the following questions to guide your conversations and to invite feedback about your words and interpretations.

1. What judgments did you make about the event? Yourself? Others?

2. To what extent did you create possibility or close it off with your choice of words?

3. What actions did you take, and what informed your actions?

4. What were the results of your actions?

5. Did your actions create possibility?

What you may have found in doing this exercise is that you have fallen into a trap of thinking there is only one "truth" in your story. Welcome to being human. That's the good news. The bad news is that your story may be causing you and others around you to suffer. What would happen if you could see other truths? How would embracing other possibilities have changed the actions you took?

Right Speech

Embracing possibilities is endlessly giving. In Eastern philosophy, there is a concept called "right speech," which is fundamental to creating possibility with the words that you use. The guidelines of right speech include the following:

BE TRUTHFUL. When speaking to someone, speak the truth as you know it. Caution: do not claim to know "the truth."

BE USEFUL. When giving someone feedback, be sure that what you are saying will be useful to the listener. For example, it does no good to tell a short person that he or she would be better off as a tall person.

BE KIND. Be sure your words are kind, not hostile; compassionate, not judgmental; roomy, not intended to box someone in.

BE UNIFYING. Be sure that your intention is to sustain the relationship or bring yourself closer to the person, not the other way around.

There are times in life when you may not be treated well by others, when your angry reaction may be appropriate, and where you skillfully need to speak up about being mistreated. We are not saying "accept it all" and do nothing. We are saying that it is important to notice how you react to what happens in your life and to make choices that create possibility rather than limit it. So, you can recognize that your anger is worth honoring and allow it to point you to better options to handling a situation productively. Rather than passively accepting injustice, find a way to alleviate it and raise the standards by which you and the rest of us live. Your awareness of self is your most powerful tool for creating a world of possibilities, which starts with you and spreads out to others—to groups, to communities, and eventually to the world. As Margaret Mead said, "don't think that a small group of committed citizens cannot change the world...indeed, it is the only thing that ever has."

Your Desires

There are two broad types of desire. One type is wholesome desire. This includes things like the desire to be happy, to make a difference, to be peaceful, and the desire for harmony with others. The consequence of a wholesome desire is that no person or thing is harmed in the achievement of it.

The second type is unwholesome desire. Some cultures promote unwholesome desires such as the desire for more things, more money, more success, more of everything. This hunger for more leads to negative consequences including damage to the natural environment, stress, competition, turf battles, addictions and emotional suffering. Upon examination of their own desires, many people discover that unwholesome desires are running their life. *Such desires can never be satisfied.*

Ask yourself, "What do I want? What is it I desire—in my life, in this situation?"* But don't stop there. Go the next step and honestly ask yourself if this is a wholesome or an unwholesome desire. Will the satisfaction of this desire lead to positive or negative consequences?

Criteria For Wholesome Desires

If your answer to the following questions is "no," you probably have a wholesome desire.

Will the fulfillment of this desire…

- ❏ Harm you or anyone else?

- ❏ Harm the environment or anyone's property?

- ❏ Lead to greed, anger, or hatred?

- ❏ Create more distance between you and your loved ones?

- ❏ Lead to more desire?

---

* For more information on exploring your life purpose, read *Finding Your Purpose: A Guide to Personal Fulfillment* by Barbara Braham, Crisp Series.

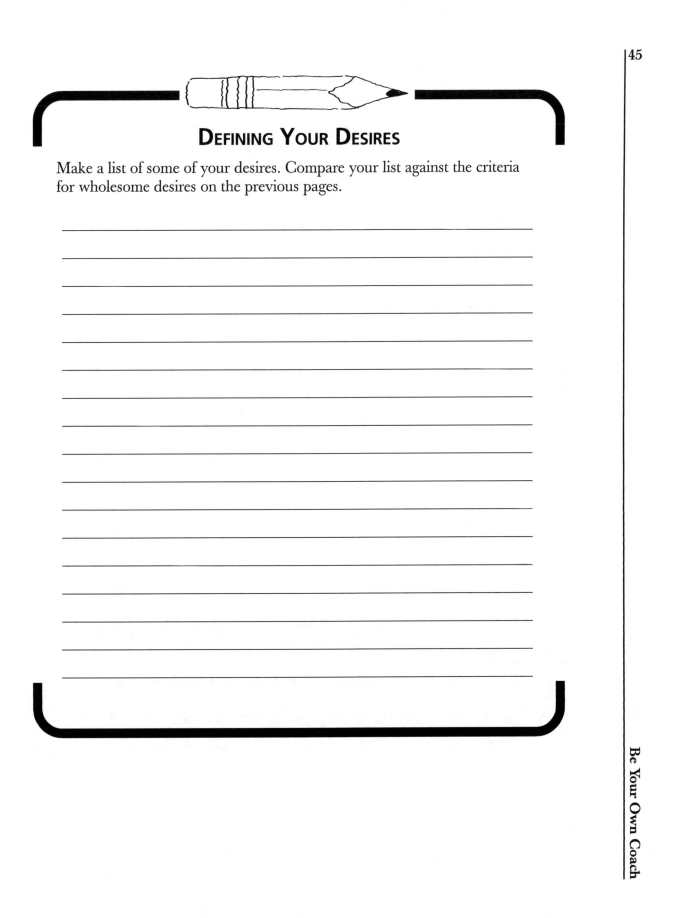

DEFINING YOUR DESIRES

Make a list of some of your desires. Compare your list against the criteria for wholesome desires on the previous pages.

Your Intentions

Behind every action there is an intention. Intentions are as important as actions. You don't move your body without first having an intention to move. Most of the time this happens so quickly that you are unaware of the intention that precedes the movement. You can experiment with this right now. Begin with the intention to touch your forefinger to your nose. If you pay close attention you will notice that your body begins to move as soon as you set the intention.

Intention makes all the difference. Imagine a supervisor who gives one of her workers a new job assignment. What is the intention? Does she want to stretch the employee into new learning? Or does she want the employee to fail so she will feel justified in firing her?

The action in these two situations is the same. An employee is given a new job assignment. But the intention is completely different. In one case the intention is for development and growth; in the other the intention is to set someone up to fail.

Where are your actions coming from? Is your intention to satisfy wholesome or unwholesome desires?

Do you intend to:

❑ Get your share *or* see to it that everyone can benefit?

❑ Make sure you get your way *or* do you want a win-win outcome?

❑ Impress others with what you know, *or* do you want to share your knowledge?

❑ Provide a flexible structure *or* do you intend to control things?

❑ Express your views *or* do you intend to intimidate others into going along with you?

CONSIDER YOUR INTENTIONS

Go back to the opening you identified on page 6, Your Coaching Opportunities. What are your intentions in this situation? Be honest with yourself. Most people give little conscious thought to their intentions. If you want to coach yourself, you need to tell yourself the truth about your motivations.

With a coaching partner, have a conversation about what your intention has been as you've completed the exercises together so far. Was your intention to look good? Learn? Self-disclose? Experiment with new behaviors? Has your intention influenced how you are interacting with your coaching partner?

Your Actions

You can have the best of intentions, yet good intentions are insufficient to get the outcome you want. You also need skillful actions. Your intention may be to express how you feel to your boss about being asked to work late. If you lack the verbal skills to express how you feel, you may come across as critical or blaming. Instead of resolving the situation, your words may make it worse.

As your own coach, you need to learn to distinguish between your intentions and your actions. You need to evaluate whether you aren't getting the results you want because of your intentions or because of unskillful actions. If your intentions are wholesome, and your skills are lacking or underdeveloped, you may want to look for a training course to expand those skills.

Your Beliefs

Finally, you need to add the lens of beliefs to your kaleidoscope. Nearly 100 years ago Henry Ford said, "If you think you can, or you think you can't, you're right." Those words remain true in the 21ˢᵗ century.

Your beliefs shape the way you see the world. They determine how you view a situation. Some beliefs will open you, others will close you down. When you're feeling stuck in your life, ask yourself what beliefs are being triggered. Are those beliefs serving you?

Below is a list of empowering beliefs held by many people who are professional coaches. If you intend to coach yourself, it is important that you know how your beliefs line up against the beliefs of professional coaches. If you find it difficult to accept these basic beliefs, you may want to hire a coach to guide you through an inquiry into your beliefs.

Coaching Beliefs

➤ People can change

➤ People can learn and become more competent

➤ People can self correct

➤ Every behavior is useful in some context

➤ All behavior makes sense within the context of a person's life interpretation

➤ People are already in the middle of many commitments

➤ The map is not the territory

➤ There is no failure, only feedback

➤ Our words create our world

➤ People have choices

PUT YOUR BREAKDOWN UNDER THE KALEIDOSCOPE

Identify a breakdown you have been facing recently, then answer the questions that follow here or in your journal to help you understand the kaleidoscope approach.

My breakdown:

1. What are the facts of your breakdown? _____

_____

2. What are your feelings? _____

_____

3. What mood do you bring to this breakdown? _____

_____

4. What words and interpretations are you using to describe your breakdown? _____

_____

5. What are your desires? Are they wholesome or unwholesome? _____

_____

6. What are your intentions? _____

_____

7. What actions have you tried? _____

_____

8. What are your beliefs? _____

_____

With a coaching partner

PUT YOUR BREAKDOWN UNDER THE KALEIDOSCOPE

Interview your partner about his/her breakdown using the preceding questions. What new insights surface as a result of this thoughtful reflection? Do any new possibilities for action show up for either of you as a result of your conversation?

The Only Way Out Is Forward

Now that you have viewed your coaching opportunity through the kaleidoscope, you're ready to take action. It is common to want to do something–anything! There is a feeling that if you take any action you will be making progress. But that is not true. Often, the action you take is like sitting in a rocking chair. There is motion, but you aren't getting anywhere.

Agitation

Reactive action seems most common in Western cultures, and reflects agitation, not movement. Agitation results from feeling anxious. It takes place in the external world and frequently leads to busyness. You find yourself without any personal time due to professional, community, or personal commitments. At the end of the day you fall into bed exhausted. There is no time to think about your life, or what you deeply want for yourself. In essence, you've distracted yourself from taking meaningful action to respond to the coaching opening you are facing. When your actions come from agitation they have a frenetic, time-compressed quality to them.

Movement

Movement, on the other hand, takes place on the inside. An inner shift leads to new and different actions. Movement may occur when you see something from a different perspective, change a belief, or let go of something that may have been true but is no longer true. Movement occurs when you see yourself in a new way, and leads to actions that are solid and grounded in the place of inner stillness.

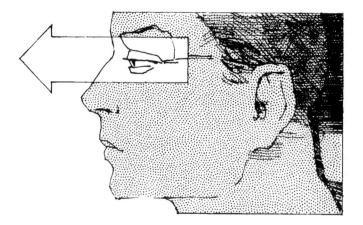

Four Stages of Movement

Movement happens when you work through and honor a process. In the case of coaching, there are four stages you will pass through on your journey to being more fully who you are. Movement occurs as a result of entering each stage, completing the work of that stage, and leaving it to enter the next stage. The process will deepen and expand you.

STAGE 1
Letting Go

STAGE 4
Looking Back to Realize You Moved Forward

STAGE 2
Living with the Question

STAGE 3
Exploring New Beginnings

STAGE **1** Letting Go

In this stage you realize that something in your life is not working as you want it to. There is something you need to let go. Perhaps you need to let go of a relationship, or the number of hours you work, or the expectation you had about attaining a certain position by a certain age. Or maybe you need to let go of certain beliefs about the world. Whatever it may be, the first stage following a breakdown is to let go and acknowledge a loss. In fact, the loss may be what is triggering your breakdown.

STAGE **2** Living with the Question

For many people, this is the most difficult stage because there are no answers yet and things feel ambiguous and uncertain. Many people want to skip this stage and jump into action, but remember: hasty action leads to agitation rather than movement. Instead, get comfortable with ambiguity and "not knowing."

If you look at the word "question," you see that it contains within it the essence of this second stage: Quest -I-On. What quest are you on? If you are willing to live with your question, you will discover that the question changes with time. It ripens. And, if you cultivate it, something fresh can emerge.

For example, your question might be: "Do I want to accept a position as team leader?" At first glance, this is a question with a "yes" or "no" answer. But if you live with the question, you may discover it holds within it these deeper questions:

> *"What does it mean to me to be a leader?"*
>
> *"What are my professional aspirations?"*
>
> *"If I say 'yes' what will I need to say 'no' to as a result of that 'yes'?"*
>
> *"Why would I want to be a team leader? What would my 'yes' say? That I look successful? I want more power? I want to serve others?"*
>
> *"Why wouldn't I want to be a team leader? What does my 'no' say? I am afraid of responsibility? I don't believe in myself and don't want more stress? I want time with my family?"*

Our culture places a great deal of emphasis on "knowing the answer," but how open to learning are you if you already know? Developing yourself requires a willingness to be *curious*, to *not know*. One of the greatest teachers of all times was Socrates. His method of teaching is known as the Socratic method, which consists of asking questions. The greatest inventors and thinkers make their contribution to the world as a result of the questions they ask.

STAGE 3 Exploring New Beginnings

Your new questions will lead to new possibilities and new futures. In this stage, you step outside of what you have always done and allow yourself to explore. You may read new types of books, or take courses or seminars that you'd never thought of before. You might look into a new hobby or sport, or commit yourself to developing new relationships with people who haven't previously been in your life. Or your explorations may be subtler. You might explore the impact of intention on the quality of your day. You might experiment with making requests of people for what you want.

This is a time of both learning *and unlearning*. Dee Hock, the founder of Visa International said, "We can't discard mental 'stuff.' But we can create a mental attic and put a sign on the door that says, 'Things I know that are no longer so.'"

Perhaps you've always planned everything in your life, whether you were at work or at home. During the phase of living with the question, you may have discovered that your urge to plan comes from a desire to control life. In the exploration stage, you begin to explore different ways of relating to the world and you decide to experiment with spontaneity. You might take a weekend trip without making advance plans for where you will stay or where you will eat. You let the weekend unfold and observe yourself. Are you relaxed and comfortable? Or do you feel anxious and tense? What happens?

New beginnings can take courage, It takes courage to move from what you know to what is new for you. Yet, you've probably heard all this before: you rely too much on your strengths, and they can become your weaknesses. Consider this case study.

56

CASE STUDY: JOHANNA

Johanna was very successful in her job as a team leader. She was clearly in charge. She was very good at seeing the big picture, and loved the power and limelight of her position.

When the organization underwent a major change that flattened the management hierarchy, her position was no longer needed. In fact, team leaders were a thing of the past. Self-directed teams took over. Johanna applied for what looked like a plum position on a team since she wanted to continue to be powerful and influence others.

Johanna's strength in the past was to take a stand, take charge, give orders, and never back down. This often worked. But in this new, flatter organization, Johanna's hard-charging style no longer worked. For her to succeed at this new position, she needed to learn a new way of being. Giving orders and making demands created distance and resistance. Yet even though her approach didn't work, she did what many of us do...she tried harder, spoke louder, demanded more. Her approach didn't change. Eventually, she began to suffer and started looking for another job.

In the case study above, Johanna's strength became her weakness. As things changed around her, she refused to change. Trying harder didn't work. She went for the quick fix of finding a new place to work. Sometimes this is a reasonable thing to do, but sometimes the best thing to do is to view the changes around you as your chance to develop and stretch parts of yourself that so far have been underutilized. If she had been able to respond to the changes by developing her interpersonal skills, she may have succeeded in the new organization.

If you want to be promoted, acquire new responsibilities, or otherwise expand your work, it is required that you create ways to continually develop yourself. Today's organizations have a vested interest in keeping great employees, and the way to stay valuable to your employer is to continually be learning about yourself and developing yourself in new ways.

A GOOD STRETCH

First:

Answer these questions in the space provided, or in your journal.

1. What am I really good at?

_____

_____

2. How have I been rewarded for being good at this?

_____

_____

3. How is this strength limiting me?

_____

_____

4. What can I develop in myself to stretch myself and expand my skills?

_____

_____

(CONTINUED)

(CONTINUED)

Next:

Without stopping, take ten minutes to write freely about how your strengths have served you, and how they may be limiting to you. There are no right or wrong answers here. The aim of writing is to tap into your inner wisdom. In doing this exercise, you will get some clues into how your strengths serve you and limit you.

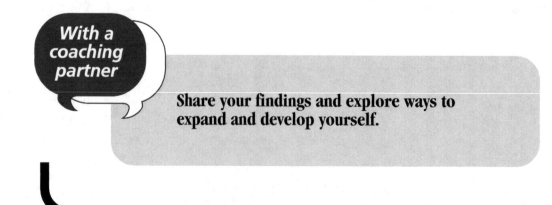

With a coaching partner

Share your findings and explore ways to expand and develop yourself.

STAGE 4 Looking Back To Realize You Have Moved Forward

The coaching process is organic, and it can be subtle. There may not be a single, distinct moment when you are "different" or "changed." The change is the accumulation of many different moments. There will be a point, however, when you can look back and see that you are no longer where you were or who you were.

This is the value of reflection. By taking time out on a regular basis, you can see where you were and where you are now. It is through reflection you become aware of changes that have taken place.

An example of this would be if you have ever suffered a loss. Perhaps you were grieving the loss of a loved one, or a job, or some aspect of your health. You experienced many days of sadness and began to fear you would always be sad. Then, there was a moment of reflection when you realized that the sadness had eased. You didn't feel the same heaviness. There was more space around the grief and you realized, "I'm better."

There wasn't any distinct moment when you were better. Instead, there was a gradual change that could be seen after it had accumulated. It is like the weight of a snowflake. We think of a snowflake as weightless, but if you have been in a climate with snow you know that there is a moment when one snowflake added to a branch covered with other "weightless" snowflakes is sufficient to break off an entire branch. It is the same with reflection: Your changes may be so gradual that they have to accumulate to a point that they are visible to you. Reflection is a tool to recognize movement in your life.

REFLECTING

Which of the four stages are you in? Check (✔) one.

❑ Stage 1: Letting Go

❑ Stage 2: Living with the Question

❑ Stage 3: Exploring New Beginnings

❑ Stage 4: Looking Back To Realize You Have Moved Forward

What will you need to let go? What have you let go? _____

_____

_____

What is the question you're living with? _____

_____

_____

How has the question changed over time? _____

_____

_____

What's new in your life as a result of this process? _____

_____

_____

Where have you changed as a result of this process? _____

_____

_____

With a coaching partner

Share your answers to the previous exercise with each other. Use the following questions to reflect on your conversation.

Are you in the same or different stages? _____

_____

_____

Which stage has opened you to the most possibilities? _____

_____

_____

Which stage has been the most difficult for you and why? If you're currently in a difficult stage, brainstorm ways that may help you move through it, people who can help you, and other sources of support.

_____

_____

Reflect on previous openings you've faced. Do you notice a pattern around which stages are easier or more difficult? What might this teach you about future challenges that occur in your life?_____

_____

_____

In summary, each of these stages is critical to your ability to create purposeful movement in your life. While you may want to speed up the process, it's best if you allow yourself to go through each stage, taking as much time as it needs. Let the stage "work you"—not the other way around.

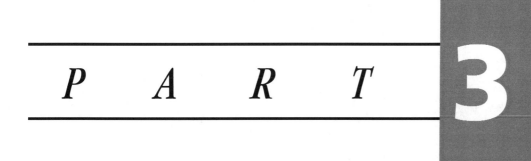

PART 3

The Coach's Toolbox

Seven Tools for Achieving Breakthroughs

The kaleidoscope approach to your coaching opening described in Part 2 helps you see your situation from a variety of perspectives. In the same way, you need a variety of approaches to choose from when you respond to your coaching situation. Not every tool will be appropriate in your situation. By using a combination of these tools, you can gain a variety of perspectives on how to address your coaching opening. For example, through a process of inquiry you might identify one plan of action, but through self-observation you might see a completely different set of possibilities. This section will introduce you to coaching tools that you can use to learn the most from your coaching opportunity.

These seven tools hold the possibility to lead to a breakthrough in your coaching situations:

1. **Choice Management**

2. **Moving to New Domains**

3. **Self-Inquiry**

4. **Self-Observation**

5. **Practices**

6. **Commitment**

7. **Powerful Conversations and Effective Requests**

TOOL **1** Choice Management

There is a simple law of cause and effect: the choices you make lead to the outcomes you get. Wise choices lead to more desirable outcomes than unwise choices. What we sometimes fail to realize is that the wise choices may be ones that we need to invent or create.

Everyday you are bombarded with choices. For example, how many choices do you have for breakfast cereal? There is something to be learned from the people who make breakfast cereal—they have done a careful study of different people and realized their need to provide a variety of choices. Are *you* as conscientious about presenting a variety of choices to yourself when it comes to managing your life?

If you only have one option in a situation, that is not a choice, it is a mandate. If there are two options you don't have a choice, you have a dilemma. With three or more options you have a choice. When you're stuck, it often indicates that you aren't seeing enough options. Or it can mean that the options you are seeing restrict new possibilities in your life. The following exercise will help you generate more choices and options.

Wise Choice	Unwise Choice
Does not harm	Harms you, others, or the environment
Aligns with purpose	Takes you off purpose
Aligns with vision	Distracts you from vision
Resources available	Resources unavailable
Aligned with personal values	Conflicts with personal values
Connects you to others	Distances you from others

QUESTIONS TO EXPAND YOUR CHOICES

What outcome do you want? _____

_____

What would need to exist for you to have that outcome? _____

_____

What choices would you have if you...

Were a member of the opposite sex? _____

_____

Were more assertive? _____

_____

Thought of yourself as a risk taker? _____

_____

Believed in yourself? _____

_____

Believed that others want what is best for you? _____

_____

Were willing to do things in a new way? _____

_____

Were a stranger to the situation? _____

_____

Didn't care what people would say? _____

_____

Now, create an imaginary Board of Directors. Anyone whose point of view you would like to have can be appointed to your Board. They can be people you know, people you've never met, and people who are no longer alive. Ask yourself: "What choices would the individuals on my Board of Directors see?"

QUESTIONS TO NARROW YOUR CHOICES

Sometimes, the issue isn't how to expand your choices, but rather, how to limit them. You may be feeling indecisive because you have too many choices. For example, you might be committed to personal growth but you can't decide whether to take a course of study, sign up for a seminar, or hire a coach. Being overwhelmed, you make no choice and stay where you are. If this is happening to you, you can move in the direction of making a choice using these questions:

What is a choice you are considering? _____

_____

What is the likely consequence of this choice? _____

_____

Will it harm you or anyone else? ❑ yes ❑ no

Will it bring you closer to your personal purpose? ❑ yes ❑ no

Is this choice designed to bring you closer to your vision, or is it designed as an escape? ❑ closer to vision ❑ an escape

Do you have the resources available to act on this choice (time, emotions, money)? ❑ yes ❑ no

What will you give up if you make this choice? Are you willing to give it up? _____

_____

Is it aligned with your personal values? ❑ yes ❑ no

Will this deepen your connection with people, or will it put distance between you and others? ❑ connect ❑ distance

✏️ EXPLORING YOUR OPTIONS

What are the choices available to you in a coaching situation you are facing? Make a list of at least five options.

1. _____

2. _____

3. _____

4. _____

5. _____

With a coaching partner

Go over your options and apply the guidelines to making your choice.

TOOL 2 Moving to a New Domain

If you are feeling stuck, one of the most helpful choices you can make is to move into a new domain. A domain is a sphere of activity or interest. As your own coach, the best next steps for your development (getting unstuck) may be found in an area of life that you are presently not spending any time in. You may be spending lots of time thinking and reflecting. Or, you may spend your time caught up in numerous relationships. Or, you may spend your time working too much. Or, you may be caught in a particular role, like mother, daughter, son, father, boss, to the extent that the role has become your world.

A new domain opens new possibilities to you. It is important to look at your life and see what parts you are not paying attention to. Those unexplored areas may hold the answer to the way out of your breakdown.

In the story, "The Karate Kid", young Daniel was tormented by other, bigger boys. His suffering led him to ask Mr. Miyagi, the handyman at his apartment building, who was also a karate master, to teach him how to fight. Miyagi agreed to be Daniel's mentor, and early in the relationship, Miyagi gave him some rags and asked him to wax a car. Daniel resisted because he couldn't understand why Miyagi was having him wax the car instead of teaching him to fight. What Daniel didn't understand was that Miyagi was teaching self-confidence and mind control first, which would eventually prepare Daniel to be excellent in martial arts. And, the arm movements required to wax the car were the same Daniel would eventually use in defending himself.

Miyagi understood the concept of learning something through a different domain. Daniel wanted to learn to fight, but Miyagi assigned him seemingly unrelated tasks that built his confidence, his stick-to-itiveness, and his strength. This worked in the story, and it can work in your life.

EXPLORING NEW DOMAINS

Moving to a new domain often creates immediate gains as well as new learning that you can take back into your life to create different outcomes. So, get out of the pool you normally swim in! When something is keeping you stuck, don't stay there, go somewhere else.

For example, let's say that you are working too hard and feeling stress. Recently, you've been passed over for promotion, or your boss has been harsh to you, or a high-visibility project you've been working on is no longer important. You are angry and can't get past the anger (consumed by an emotion). When these things happen, most people focus on ways to cope. You may find yourself withdrawing, feeling uncomfortable, lashing out, working even harder, or recruiting others to see the situation exactly as you do.

Instead of staying angry, you could choose to deal with it by doing something new and different. You could move into a new domain. There are hundreds of ways to learn about yourself and this opening. Here are some activities in various domains that have proven to be especially useful to people:

Avtivities to Explore a New Domain		
Meditation	Yoga	Voice Lessons
Spiritual study	Painting/Drawing	Sculpting
Networking	Martial Arts	Music
Acting/Improvisation	New sport	New field of study
Cooking	Family outings	Volunteering
Dancing	Hospice work	Metaphor-Making

BRAINSTORMING

Use the following questions to brainstorm ways you can learn through a new domain.

1. What did you love to do when you were younger that you no longer have time to do? _____

_____

2. In which of these domains do you spend most of your time?

❏ the world of work—work is your major focus

❏ the world of information—learning about things and working with things are your major focus

❏ the role(s) you are in—your role is your major focus

❏ the world of relationships—your relationships with people are your major focus

❏ the world of creation—creating ideas or things are your major focus

❏ the world of reflection—thinking and introspecting are your major focus

3. When you have identified where you spend most of your time, choose one of the other areas and brainstorm possible activities to engage in related to that domain.

4. Choose one activity to follow through on. If possible, link the activity back to question #1, something you loved to do when you were younger but no longer do now.

USING METAPHORS

Entering a new domain doesn't always mean doing something new like taking on a new sport. You can enter a new domain using a metaphor.

Here are some examples of metaphors:

➤ You are a dog who has lived in the same backyard for many years. While you would love to know what's on the other side of the fence, you have decided that it is best for you if you just stay where you are.

➤ You are a graceful brightly painted front porch, inviting others to sit with you.

➤ You are a strong mountain peak, able to see above the clouds and withstand wind and weather.

A metaphor is an image that describes a situation with texture, color, and feeling. Metaphors are often a "path in" to understand a situation more deeply, and they may also offer a "path out" to see a new way of being.

For example, using the dog metaphor as a "path in" offers a picture of someone who is afraid to try something new. A "path out" metaphor might be to envision a happy pooch roaming the neighborhood, noticing new smells, finding new playgrounds (a pond, a creek, an open field) and new people to play with.

It is easy to see that if you feel stuck in your job you could identify with the dog metaphor; and the new image of a purposeful wandering pooch is one that could empower you to move out of the boundaries you have accepted for so long.

With a coaching partner

CREATING METAPHORS

While metaphor-making is often thought of as an intuitive process, anyone can learn to create metaphors. An easy way to start is to begin making analogies, by linking yourself to familiar objects around you. Once you have done that, you can make connections between yourself and things that matter to you.

Coach each other through the metaphor-making process by asking the questions below.

1. **Think of three objects that you love.**

    Object #1: _____

    Object #2: _____

    Object #3: _____

2. **Taking turns, partners ask:**

    ➤ **How is this object a representation of you?**

    ➤ **In what ways are you like the object?**

    ➤ **What qualities do you appreciate in the object?**

    ➤ **In what ways do these qualities serve you?**

    ➤ **In what ways could they serve you better?**

    ➤ **In what ways do you express these qualities every day?**

Once you have practiced making metaphors from familiar objects you can create metaphors for specific situations you are in.

Metaphors used in this way are meant to be a guide, and they are only meant to open you to possibilities that you may not have considered before. They are not a "conclusion" about yourself, and, even more important, they are not you. They are simply a window into a dilemma, a question, or a situation, and are especially useful in helping you to get "unstuck" and into a *new way of seeing and being.*

TOOL 3 Self-Inquiry

The questions you ask yourself about your story will either keep you stuck in the story, or they will create new openings for you to change your story. You have no doubt had the experience of being worried or concerned about a situation and the same thoughts rolled through your mind again and again. Likewise, the same questions will roll through your mind unless you make a conscious effort to ask yourself powerful questions.

To find new insights into your situation, you engage in a process of self-inquiry. Often when you ask yourself a question, all you really want is "an answer." As soon as you have one, the questioning stops. However, in the process of self-inquiry, you aren't satisfied with "an answer." You want to look more deeply than that. You need to find the deeper truth in the situation, which requires you to ask yourself a great variety of questions.

Questions that will help lead you towards the truth rather than just an answer are those which:

❏ Take you into a place of exploration and possibility, revealing new answers and perspectives that you hadn't anticipated.

❏ Stimulate your curiosity about yourself and your situation, taking you into a place of self-discovery.

❏ Do not provide an easy answer, but rather require you to take time, perhaps even hours or days.

❏ Deepen your awareness about yourself and/or your situation; the more aware you become, the more options you have available to you.

❏ Lead you to another question. If your question takes you to a dead end immediately, there isn't much room for learning, discovery or exploration.

YOUR IMPORTANT QUESTIONS

Write out the questions that you are asking yourself right now in your situation.

1. _____
   _____

2. _____
   _____

3. _____
   _____

4. _____
   _____

5. _____
   _____

QUESTIONS TO MOVE YOU FORWARD

Here are some examples of questions that you could use in the self-inquiry process:

➤ Who would I need to be to get what I want?

➤ What is one thing that I could do right now that would make a difference in how I'm feeling about the situation?

➤ What am I tolerating?

➤ What way of seeing this situation am I attached to or defending?

➤ What is waiting for expression?

➤ What resources are available to me that I'm not using in this situation?

➤ What is the essential pain in this situation that I need to bear?

➤ How am I avoiding my feelings?

➤ Who am I in this situation? Who do I want to be?

➤ What am I withholding?

➤ Am I moving into or away from my fears?

➤ Is this something I need to accept? Or is it a situation where I need to take action?

➤ How could I be kind to myself?

➤ What do I fear I'll have to give up?

➤ What am I afraid of saying "yes" to and what am I afraid of saying "no" to?

➤ What am I overlooking?

➤ What am I afraid other people will say about me?

➤ What would allow me to move forward if I completed it?

➤ What conversation am I afraid to have?

➤ What am I not admitting to myself?

YOUR IMPORTANT QUESTIONS REVISITED

Now go back to your list of questions on page 76, and in the space below,
either rewrite them or create five new questions that would take you into the
place of inquiry regarding the situation you are in.

1. _____

   _____

2. _____

   _____

3. _____

   _____

4. _____

   _____

5. _____

   _____

With a coaching partner

Brainstorm other questions you could ask
yourself around your specific openings.
Notice how the quality of the questions you
ask leads you to a deeper place of inquiry.

TOOL 4 Self-Observation

Do any of the following sound like something you would say?

"I always listen to the other person's viewpoint."

"I am open to what others have to say."

"I look for the good, the positive, in every situation."

"I follow through on my commitments."

"I like to be fair to everyone."

There is often a gap between what we think we do, the way we think we behave, and what we actually do. Often, when there is a coaching opportunity, what you *think* you are doing and what you *actually* are doing are different. Paying attention to your own behaviors is necessary for effective coaching.

CASE STUDY: JIM

Jim was a high energy, go-getter who liked to have his ideas heard. When he had an idea, he pushed to get it aired, and in that process he left no space for conversation. But he did not realize that he was doing this. He confided to his boss that others didn't seem to support his ideas, and he couldn't understand why they didn't offer suggestions.

His boss suggested to him that there seemed to be little room for any ideas other than his own. Jim disagreed, so his boss challenged him to do a self-observation exercise. They agreed that every time he presented an idea, Jim would watch for two things:

➤ **What ideas did he get from anyone else in the conversation (i.e., was he as open as he thought he was)?**

➤ **What actions did he take when he felt like he was losing ground?**

The boss had a hunch that Jim heard no one else's ideas, and that when people shut down around him, he talked louder and faster.

Jim returned to his boss a week later to report on his self-observation exercise. Much to his surprise, he learned that his boss was right. He created little or no space for others, people did shut down, and when they did, he became pushy, talked louder, and even argued.

After that experience, he was ready to behave in a different way. Without doing a self-observation exercise, he would never have believed that he needed to change his way of presenting ideas. In fact, no amount of convincing would have worked. *He had to see it himself.*

HOW TO OBSERVE YOURSELF

There are so many things about our behaviors that are worthy of self-observation. Some examples follow. As you read them, think about where you might like to start.

You could observe how you:

➤ listen, or don't listen

➤ pause, or push forward

➤ state, or don't state, your feelings

➤ manage, or don't manage, your time

➤ interact with, or avoid, authority figures

➤ interact, or don't interact, with the opposite sex

➤ interact, or don't, with people who are the same sex as you

➤ notice your feelings during interactions with others

➤ notice the way your body reacts, or doesn't react, in certain situations

➤ act as a friend to your friends

➤ judge, or don't judge, others

➤ generate reactions in others

➤ make a point

➤ are affected by your emotions

Five Steps to Better Self-Observation

STEP 1: Identify a coaching opening you want to know more about.

STEP 2: Make a list of questions about how you behave in that situation. Create questions that will help you see your situation more clearly. (Refer to the previous section for guidelines on how to write your questions.)

STEP 3: Split yourself into halves. One half is your *Engaged* Self, the part of you that is in the action. The other half is your *Observer* Self, the part of you that watches yourself. The first time you try this you may find it a bit of a challenge, but with practice, you will be able to access your Observer Self quite easily.

STEP 4: Re-enter your coaching situation. Have your Observer Self watch your Engaged Self using the questions you created in Step 2.

STEP 5: Record what you learn in your journal.

With a coaching partner

SELF-OBSERVATION PRACTICE

1. **Think of a coaching opening that occurs for you. Write it down.**

_____

_____

2. **Write down a hunch you have about what might be useful to observe.**

_____

_____

3. **Create some questions that will help you to look at yourself.**

_____

_____

4. **Each day for at least a week, observe yourself in the situation you have identified. Notice what you do AND how you feel, including where the feelings show up in your body.**

5. **At the end of each day, use your journal to write your ideas and responses to the questions you created.**

At the end of each week, look over what you have written and have a conversation with your coaching partner about the following questions:

"What have I learned about myself this week?"

"What can I do differently based on what my findings tell me?"

You may begin to notice that some of what you do is habitual and is linked to your view of the world. What you do may also be linked to what has worked for you in the past. For example, a breakdown is a signal that it is time to learn a _new way of seeing and being_. Anytime you are in a breakdown situation or a situation where you want to change your behavior, use self-observation exercises to learn about where you are. This is the best way to identify new actions and ways of thinking and being that will serve you better.

TOOL 5 Practices

What is a practice? A practice is an activity that you do repeatedly to awaken and deepen some part of yourself. For example, a soccer coach holds a practice so that the team members can work on becoming more competent in their foot work, kicks, ball handling, and strategy. During soccer practice, the goal is not to see how many times a player can kick. Rather, a practice is for team members to learn more about what they are doing: what they do with their left foot, their right foot, their eyes, their shoulders, hips, and body. Soccer coaches create drills that the players do *over and over* to learn what they are doing and how they can do it better.

A *practice* is different from a *discipline*. While you need the discipline of a commitment, a time, a place, and frequency to begin a practice, the discipline is not the practice. Discipline has to do with self-control and maintaining a routine. It brings with it a certain rigidity. Practice has to do with self-awareness and learning. Below is a chart that distinguishes the two.

Discipline	Practice
Done because you should do it	Done because you wish to learn and raise awareness
Done with a goal in mind	Done with a purpose in mind, but not a goal
Done according to certain standards	Done with structures, but not according to any specific standards of right/wrong
Done just to do it or because it is	Done with awareness and intention to learn
Tool for getting something done	Tool for change and transformation
Based on will, constriction, achievement	Based on desire, expansion, love

The Discipline/Practice Distinction

Another example may help you see the difference between discipline and practice. Let's say that you want to be a better supervisor. You want to be seen as caring and fair. If you are disciplined about it, your choices may look like this:

Discipline:

➤ Every day, spend 10 minutes walking through your department making sure you say hello to everyone.

➤ Once a month, have a wind-down gathering on a Friday afternoon.

➤ Every week, visit a department to observe how people are working.

And that's the end of it. What are others getting out of it? A little more face time with you, but that is it. Now, look at a practice for the same thing.

Practice:

➤ Every day, spend time walking through your department and making sure you say hello to everyone. Listen to what is up with people and find ways to learn their concerns. Find out what they love about work. Follow up on what you learn by addressing concerns promptly.

➤ Once a month, have a wind-down gathering on a Friday afternoon. Listen for the energy in the room. Listen for the stories, the successes, the fun that your group of subordinates and colleagues offer. Notice how you react in the situation. What draws you in? What keeps you engaged? What is your part in that?

➤ Every week, visit a department to observe how people are working. Engage in conversations and learn about what excites, what motivates, what discourages. Give of yourself. Notice your reactions and thoughts.

If you are engaged in the practice of being a better supervisor, then you are deepening the relationship that you have with the people you work with by learning what matters to them. You are also learning about yourself—your patience, your listening, and your ability to see the world through their eyes.

Five Steps to Designing a Practice for Yourself

STEP 1: Self-observe. Start by gathering data about how you are being in a particular situation, what works and what doesn't work.

STEP 2: Set a goal. What do you want to change? Learn more about? Deepen?

STEP 3: Create a practice that you can do often (at least once a day). Stick with this practice for a specific period of time, such as a month. Practices can be about a change of behavior, a change in your self-talk, a change in your interpretations, and so on.

STEP 4: Reflect. At the end of each day, set aside 10 minutes to write down what you learned about yourself. Or have a conversation with your coaching partner about what you learned.

STEP 5: Self-correct. At the end of the month, fine tune your practice, or create a new one.

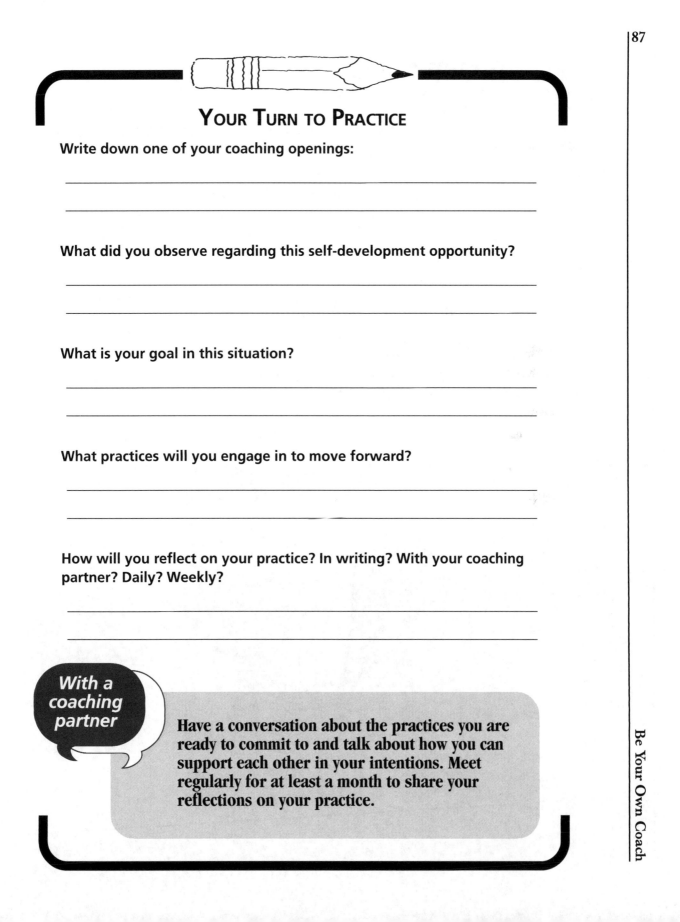

YOUR TURN TO PRACTICE

Write down one of your coaching openings:

_____

_____

What did you observe regarding this self-development opportunity?

_____

_____

What is your goal in this situation?

_____

_____

What practices will you engage in to move forward?

_____

_____

How will you reflect on your practice? In writing? With your coaching partner? Daily? Weekly?

_____

_____

With a coaching partner

Have a conversation about the practices you are ready to commit to and talk about how you can support each other in your intentions. Meet regularly for at least a month to share your reflections on your practice.

TOOL 6 Commitment

You can create as many practices as you want, but it takes commitment to do them. Without a commitment, any change that you are intending to make is less likely to occur.

Once you begin to see through your story and its limiting beliefs, you also begin to see new options and possibilities. You will forever be in the "thinking about the options" stage unless you actually make a commitment and say, "I am committed to being a better supervisor (colleague, leader, speaker, parent, sister, brother, etc.)."

Commitment begins internally, and it is the result of all the work you have done to identify what would help to make your life better. *Unlike a goal, which sets a direction, a commitment is a pledge to a course of action you make to yourself.* It is always about something that really matters. It is always about achieving a new way of being. Whatever you wish to achieve will happen when you make a clear commitment followed by actions to support it.

Five Steps for Making Commitments

STEP 1: Envision and define an outcome. Write out your commitment. Stephen R. Covey, author of *7 Habits of Highly Successful People*, says, "Begin with the end in mind."

STEP 2: Determine what support you need to keep your commitment. What can help you? Who can help you? What do you need to keep or eliminate in your life in order to keep your commitment? What do you need to say "yes" to and what do you need to say "no" to? Decide what actions you will take to honor your commitment.

STEP 3: Let selected others know what you are up to. Decide who can offer you genuine support and request support from those people. As you begin fulfilling your commitment, you can tell more people what you are doing.

STEP 4: Keep track in your journal of how you are doing with regard to the commitment. Write about what actions you are taking, what reactions you are getting, how you are managing those reactions, and what you need to do or say to yourself to keep yourself on track.

STEP 5: Celebrate your successes. When you have fulfilled your commitment, honor your process and celebrate!

YOUR TURN TO COMMIT

1. Envision an outcome to a current coaching opening.

2. Write out your commitment. _____

_____

_____

3. What will be the biggest obstacle(s) to keeping your commitment?

_____

_____

4. What support do you need to keep your commitment? What, or who, can help you? _____

_____

_____

5. What do you need to say "yes" to? _____

_____

6. What do you need to say "no" to? _____

_____

With a coaching partner

Tell your partner what your commitment is. Talk with each other about what you will need to do to honor your commitment, brainstorming sources of support beyond your partnership, and make requests of each other for support. Check in with each other weekly to support each other's intention regarding your commitments.

TOOL 7 Powerful Conversations and Effective Requests

Most people *talk*, but simply "talking" is a superficial form of communicating that floats along the surface without making contact between you and the other person. While most information exchange takes place at the level of *talk*, so also does most mindless chatter.

Speaking is different. When you speak, you come from a place of silence. You are connected with yourself and that makes it possible to connect with the other person.

Powerful Conversations

Conversation occurs when two or more people are *speaking*. When a real conversation takes place, it stays with you long after the exchange of words has ended. James Hillman, author of *The Soul's Code: In Search of Character and Calling* (NY: Warner Books, 1997) writes:

"Not just any talk is conversation, not any talk raises consciousness. A subject can be talked to death, a person talked to sleep. Good conversation has an edge: it opens your eyes to something, quickens your ears. And good conversation reverberates: it keeps on talking in your mind later in the day; the next day you find yourself still talking with what was said. That reverberation afterwards is the very raising of consciousness: your mind's been moved."

In order to be your own coach, you need to become skillful in two types of conversations:

➤ **Conversations of Possibility**

➤ **Conversations of Action**

Conversations of Possibility

These are conversations in which you create your future. You explore what is possible for you. You declare what you want. These are the conversations that generate energy and give you a feeling of hope. At the end of a conversation of possibility, you will notice your horizons have expanded and you will actually feel bigger. Without conversations of possibility, you live your life out of your past instead of out of your future.

In conversations of possibility you'll find yourself saying things like:

"What if…"

"Imagine…"

"I could…"

"It seems impossible, but I will go for it…"

Conversations of Action

The most important conversations of action are the ones you have with yourself. It may surprise you to realize that action begins with a conversation. It is during your internal conversations that you make decisions and commitments to yourself about what you will do in the external world. *Decisions* and *commitments* are the two key terms.

When you make a *decision* to telephone a potential customer about doing business together, you have taken the first step that leads to picking up the phone and dialing that customer's number. The second step is making a *commitment* to yourself as to when you will make the call. The decision is the big picture, and the commitment is the specific step. Without the decision to call and the commitment of when you will call, the likelihood that you will ever place the call is very small.

Conversations of action can also be held with other people. The two key concepts in these conversations are *requests* and *commitments*. Continuing with the example of the sales call, let's imagine that you now have the prospect on the phone. To continue the action you will need to make a request of your prospect. Requests that you could make include: requesting an appointment, requesting that they purchase your product or service, or requesting that they refer you to someone else.

Once the request is made, your prospect has an opportunity to say "yes" or "no." If the prospect says "yes," then a commitment has been made. For example, if the prospect agrees to an appointment, they are committing to be there for the meeting. In response, you will likely make a commitment of your own. You might commit to show up at a particular time, you might commit to take a specific amount of time, you might commit to bring literature on your product or service. These two verbal acts—requests and commitments—have put you into motion.

Effective Requests

Making a request seems simple enough. You do it all the time…or do you? Many people do not get the outcomes they want because they fail to make clear, well-thought-out requests.

To make an effective request:

➤   Name exactly what you want.

➤   Specify whom you want it from.

➤   State what will create satisfaction. For example, what is the time-frame? How much money will it cost? How many people will be involved?

➤   Establish a common ground of understanding about the terminology you're using.

REQUEST OR NOT?

Decide whether the following examples meet the criteria of an effective request as described on the previous page. If so, check (✔) **yes**.
If not, check (✔) **no** and explain which component(s) are missing.

1. **"Can you help me with this project?"**

   Request? ❑ yes ❑ no

2. **"Will you fax this mileage report to our branch office this afternoon?"**

   Request? ❑ yes ❑ no

3. **"Let me know if you have any items for the meeting agenda."**

   Request? ❑ yes ❑ no

4. **"The last three meetings you led ran over their scheduled time."**

   Request? ❑ yes ❑ no

5. **"The training room is a mess!"**

   Request? ❑ yes ❑ no

6. **"Will you take notes on the action items we agree to in our team meeting and distribute them to all the members within a week?"**

   Request? ❑ yes ❑ no

1. No. Not specific. What kind of help? By when? For how long?
2. Yes. Request
3. No. Not specific. When?
4. No. Gripe, not request.
5. No. Gripe, not request.
6. Yes. Request

CONSTRUCTING BETTER REQUESTS

Go back to the coaching opportunity you described on page 6. What requests could you make to take action? Write them down.

_____

_____

_____

Next, check your requests against the components of an effective request. Are they really requests?

Note over the next few weeks how the people around you make requests and have conversations of possibility or action. Notice what moves a conversation forward and what holds it back.

Hold a 15-minute conversation of possibility with your coaching partner about the possibilities of the coaching opening you face. Notice your use of language during the conversation. Are you more in the future or in the past? Take turns with this so that each of you can explore your own possibilities.

After holding your conversation of possibility, hold a second conversation in which you create a list of at least five requests you could make to take action in the present on your possibility.

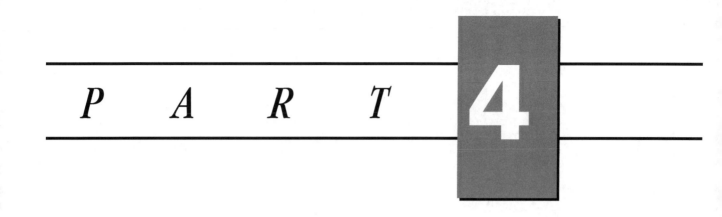

Supporting Yourself in the Coaching Process

Ways to Stay on Your New Path

You have been on a fruitful journey if you have engaged fully with the exercises in this book. How can you maintain your new perspective and stay supported in your coaching efforts? Here are some ideas.

➤ **Foster new coaching partner relationships**

➤ **Re-contract with your current coaching partner**

You can ask your coaching partner to continue to work with you. The two of you can continue to explore—using life as your palette. You can face new opportunities, create new practices, and make new commitments. You can help each other remember the learnings, the patterns, the risks, and the joys of coaching yourself towards desired outcomes.

Find a New Coaching Partner

You can tell others around you about the learning process you have just experienced. Someone else may be interested in engaging with you in this learning. A new coaching partner may offer you new perspectives and possibilities.

Create a Learning Circle

Find others who are dedicated to personal and/or professional development and create a group. Together you can explore, by using the concepts in the book, who you are and the potential in your life.

Forming a Learning Circle:

1. Decide on the purpose for the group and invite people who have a similar interest.

2. Schedule a couple of hours to get together once a month. Set a specific meeting time. Decide whether you want to include a "social" time, and if so, decide when: before you start the meeting or after.

3. Set ground rules for the group's work, such as:

   ➤ All conversations are confidential

   ➤ Statements are to be nonjudgmental, respectful, truthful, and useful

   ➤ People arrive on time and the meeting ends on time

   ➤ Listen with the heart and the mind

   ➤ Any others that you think would be helpful to the group

4. Using this book, work through one or two exercises at each meeting. Set guidelines on timing: how long to spend on each exercise, how long the sharing will be, how long any one individual may speak.

5. Choose a facilitator: it can be the same person, or you can decide to rotate this role for each meeting.

6. Optional: you may want to begin and end the meeting with a ritual, which can be as simple as a one-minute check-in and check-out, where each person makes a few comments. Or you can create a more elaborate ritual, such as lighting a candle or playing music.

For advanced groups—where the group members know the concepts in this book—you can structure your meetings around themes. For example:

➤ What *self-observation* exercises group members are engaged in

➤ What *practices* members are doing and how that is going

➤ Where people are *stuck*

➤ How to make metaphors

➤ How to recognize if your stories limit or create possibilities

There is a history of circle sharing in many cultures, including Native Americans and Quakers. If the circle idea appeals to you, you may want to read the book *Wisdom Circles: A Guide to Self-Discovery and Community Building in Small Groups,* by Charles Garfield, Cindy Spring, and Sedonia Cahill (NY: Hyperion, 1999).

Find a Professional Coach

There may be times when you need to work with an experienced professional coach, someone who can help you get past barriers. The good news is that there are many excellent coaches working with people in all sorts of industries and organizations, and you can find them by making a phone call or two. Other good news—if you have done the work in this book, you are quite coachable. You have been your own advocate in a most comprehensive, thorough, and humble way. Now it may be time to enlist the services of a professional coach to move you towards what seems impossible, which could mean a tremendous breakthrough for you.

To find a coach, you can check with human resource professionals for referrals to local coaches, as well as BeYourOwnCoach.com, or visit the website of the International Coach Federation, www.coachfederation.org. The website contains a list of coaches and their profiles.

Take a Course or a Workshop

There are numerous self-development workshops on topics ranging from managing stress to understanding your dreams; writing poetry, learning to draw, paint, or sculpt; building skills to enhance your professional and personal effectiveness; learning more about the natural world or the body. The world is *huge,* and the choices to continue learning abound!

Commit to being a lifelong learner and explore courses or workshops that will support that commitment.

Perform Self-Study

You can create your own "at home" course by reading other books about any of the topics contained in *Be Your Own Coach.*

Resources

Transitions: Making Sense of Life's Changes by William Bridges. Cambridge, MA: Perseus Books, 1980.

The Last Word on Power: Re-Invention for Leaders and Anyone Who Must Make the Impossible Happen by Tracy Goss. New York: Currency Doubleday, 1995.

The Adult Years: Mastering the Art of Self-Renewal by Frederic M. Hudson. San Francisco: Jossey-Bass, 1999.

Leadership and the Art of Conversation by Kim H. Krisco. Rocklin, CA: Prima Publishing, 1997.

"The Use of Metaphor in Coaching," by Chris Wahl and Leslie Williams in *The Art and Practice of Coaching Leaders,* National Leadership Institute. University of Maryland, 1998.

Successful Lifelong Learning by Robert L. Steinbach. Crisp Series, 2000.

Making the Most of Being Mentored by Gordon F. Shea. Crisp Series, 1999.

Adapting to Change: Making Change Work for You by Carol Kinsey Goman. Crisp Series, 1993.

Finding Your Purpose: Mastering the Art of Self-Renewal by Barbara Braham. Crisp Series, 2003.

Ways to Nurture Yourself During Your Process

Silence

You have an inner knower, an inner wisdom, an inner coach. It is important to build regular quiet time, regular silence into your daily schedule to contact that inner wisdom. Some people find silence every day by taking a walk in the woods, or in a park. Others live near a pond or a lake, and find their quiet time there. Others have a beautiful tree to gaze upon outside their office window, and take purposeful time daily to engage in daydreamy stillness. Others have developed a meditation practice, in which they focus for 20 minutes or more each day.

Resources

Stopping: How to Be Still When You Have to Keep Going by David Kundtz. Berkeley: Conari Press, 1998.

A Path with Heart: A Guide through the Perils and Promises of Spiritual Life by Jack Kornfield. New York: Bantam, 1993.

Any of Thich Nhat Hanh's books, especially *Peace Is Every Step: The Path of Mindfulness in Everyday Life*. New York: Bantam, 1992.

Wherever You Go, There You Are: Mindfulness Meditation in Everyday Life by Jon Kabat-Zinn. New York: Hyperion, 1995.

Focusing by Eugene T. Gendlin. New York: Bantam, 1982.

Journaling

Journaling is a type of stillness that invites learning through written reflection. It is not about making a travelogue version of your day. It is about writing what you observe about your practices, commitments, and breakdowns. Or you may chose to draw them or color your reflections. There aren't rules about journaling, other than that the journal reflect your journey, your quest, your questions, your heart, and your mind. It can be very satisfying to start a journaling process at the beginning of a transition or change effort, stay committed to the process, and then, when the new outcome is achieved, look back and see the learning, the determination, the doubt, and faith that occurred.

Resources

Life's Companion: Journal Writing as a Spiritual Request by Christina Baldwin. New York: Bantam, 1998.

The Artist's Way: A Spiritual Path to Higher Creativity by Julia Cameron. New York: Jeremy Tarcher, 1992.

At a Journal Workshop by Ira Progoff. New York: Dialogue House Library, 1975.

Caring For Your Body

So much of Western culture's emphasis is on the primacy of the mind, the brain, and thinking, that it has caused many people to feel that they are separate from their body. Not so! Your body holds knowledge and emotion, so it is not to be ignored or dismissed. *The body is the fundamental system that supports your actions in life.* Caring for your body is a wise choice.

What you put into your body is what fuels it. Eat wisely. Fresh, natural foods are the best. When you ingest sugar, over-processed foods, alcohol, and drugs instead of fresh foods, you are asking the river that is your bloodstream to accommodate the debris. The body's natural systems can only deal with the overload for so long without your health being affected.

Along with fresh and healthy food, your body needs water, and lots of it. Experts recommend at least eight glasses of water a day.

You have heard this before: You need to exercise regularly! Exercise may be your new domain. Find some type of exercise that will work for you and commit to it.

Lastly, your body needs rest. Our lifestyles are busier than they have ever been. Most people are sleep deprived, and this takes its toll, over time, on your body. In addition to physical rest, the body needs the mental rest that is possible when one clears the mind through meditation or other ways of being quiet.

Resources

Eight Weeks to Optimum Health: A Proven Program for Taking Full Advantage of Your Body's Natural Healing Power by Andrew Weil. New York: Random House, 1997.

An Unused Intelligence: Physical Thinking for 21ˢᵗ Century Leadership by Andy Bryner and Dawna Markova. Berkeley: Conari Press, 1996.

Women's Bodies, Women's Wisdom: Creating Physical and Emotional Health and Healing by Christiane Northrup. New York: Bantam, 1998.

Retooling on the Run: Real Change for Leaders with No Time by Stuart Heller and David Sheppard Surrenda. Berkeley: Frog Ltd., 1995.

Final Thoughts

We have presented many tools in this book. The exercises have offered you the possibility to find pathways for greater success in your life. If you have taken the time to engage your heart and mind as you've navigated through this book, you have undoubtedly learned some new things about yourself and have begun to be in the world in new ways.

As you go forward, may you experience great joy in your commitment to being a lifelong learner. You have taken courageous steps already, steps that can transform your life into the life that is closer to your dreams. We wish you well as you continue on your journey. We would like to invite you to contact us at our website, BeYourOwnCoach.com, to share your stories and successes with us, and to learn new ways to apply the concepts in the book to your life. At our website, we expand on the concepts regularly and always have something new for you to use.

Also Available

Books•Videos•Computer-Based Training Products

If you enjoyed this book, we have great news for you. There are over 200 books available in the *Crisp Fifty-Minute™ Series*. For more information visit us online at www.axzopress.com

Subject Areas Include:

Management

Human Resources

Communication Skills

Personal Development

Sales/Marketing

Finance

Coaching and Mentoring

Customer Service/Quality

Small Business and Entrepreneurship

Training

Life Planning

Writing

VERQ